DOWN THE ROAD
NEVER TRAVELLED

DOWN THE ROAD
NEVER TRAVELLED

BRIGITTE PELLERIN

Benson A Hedges

BREAKOUT EDUCATIONAL NETWORK
IN ASSOCIATION WITH
DUNDURN PRESS
TORONTO · OXFORD

Publisher: Inta D. Erwin
Editor: Amanda Stewart, First Folio Resource Group
Copy-editor: Maggie MacDonald, First Folio Resource Group
Designer: Bruna Brunelli, Brunelli Designs
Printer: Webcom

National Library of Canada Cataloguing in Publication Data

Pellerin, Brigitte, 1970–
   Down the road never travelled/by Brigitte Pellerin.

One of the 16 vols. and 14 hours of video which make up the
   underground royal commission report
Includes bibliographical references and index.
ISBN 1-55002-422-1

   1. Finance, Public—Canada. 2. Finance, Public—Canada—
Provinces. 3. Local finance—Canada. 4. Fiscal policy—Canada.
I. Title. II. Title: underground royal commission report.

HC120.C3P44 2002   336.71   C2002-902302-5

1   2   3   4   5   07   06   05   04   03

Printed and bound in Canada.
Printed on recycled paper. ❋
www.dundurn.com

Transcripts of the interviews excerpted in *Down the Road Never Travelled* can be found in *Days of Reckoning*, edited by John Wood, *On the Money Trail*, by Tim Chorney with Jay Innes, and *Secrets in High Places* by Jay Innes.

Exclusive Canadian broadcast rights for the *underground royal commission* report

intelligent television

Check your cable or satellite listings for telecast times

Visit the *urc* Web site link at:
www.ichanneltv.com

The *underground royal commission* Report

Since September 11, 2001, there has been an uneasy dialogue among Canadians as we ponder our position in the world, especially vis à vis the United States. Critically and painfully, we are re-examining ourselves and our government. We are even questioning our nation's ability to retain its sovereignty.

The questions we are asking ourselves are not new. Over the last 30 years, and especially in the dreadful period of the early 1990s, leading up to the Quebec referendum of 1995, inquiries and Royal commissions, one after another, studied the state of the country. What *is* new is that eight years ago, a group of citizens looked at this parade of inquiries and commissions and said, "These don't deal with the real issues." They wondered how it was possible for a nation that was so promising and prosperous in the early 60s to end up so confused, divided, and troubled. And they decided that what was needed was a different kind of investigation — driven from the grassroots 'bottom,' and not from the top. Almost as a provocation, this group of people, most of whom were affiliated with the award winning documentary-maker, Stornoway Productions, decided to do it themselves — and so was born the *underground royal commission*!

What began as a television documentary soon evolved into much more. Seven young, novice researchers, hired right out of university, along with a television crew and producer, conducted interviews with people in government, business, the military and in all walks of life, across the country. What they discovered went beyond anything they had expected. The more they learned, the larger the implications grew. The project continued to evolve and has expanded to include a total of 23 researchers over the last several years. The results are the 14 hours of video and 16 books that make up the first interim report of the *underground royal commission*.

So what *are* the issues? The report of the *underground royal commission* clearly shows us that regardless of region, level of government, or political party, we are operating under a wasteful system ubiquitously lacking in accountability. An ever-weakening connection between the electors and the elected means that we are slowly and irrevocably losing our right to know our government. The researchers' experiences demonstrate that it is almost impossible for a member of the public, or in most cases, even for a member of Parliament, to actually trace how our tax dollars are spent. Most disturbing is the fact that our young people have been stuck with a crippling IOU that has effectively hamstrung their future. No wonder, then, that Canada is not poised for reaching its potential in the 21st century.

The *underground royal commission* report, prepared in large part by and for the youth of Canada, provides the hard evidence of the problems you and I may long have suspected. Some of that evidence makes it clear that, as ordinary Canadians, we are every bit as culpable as our politicians — for our failure to demand accountability, for our easy acceptance of government subsidies and services established without proper funding in place, and for the disservice we have done to our young people through the debt we have so blithely passed on to them. But the real purpose of the *underground royal commission* is to ensure that we better understand how government processes work and what role we play in them. Public policy issues must be understandable and accessible to the public if they are ever to be truly addressed and resolved. The *underground royal commission* intends to continue pointing the way for bringing about constructive change in Canada.

— Stornoway Productions

14 hours of videos also available with the *underground royal commission* report.
Visit Stornoway Productions at www.stornoway.com for a list of titles.

TABLE OF CONTENTS

INTRODUCTION

Some things I will never understand.

Why is it that, no matter how hard I work, the money always goes out faster than it comes in? Who puts the caramel into the Caramilk bar? Why can't I bring my own snacks to the movies? All mysteries. And I can't begin to figure them out.

Just like government — I mean, who knows what's going on up there on Parliament Hill?

Do you understand how government works? I have studied these things for a while now, both in and out of school, and I have come to the conclusion that even though I have a general sense of how things work around Parliament Hill, I have yet to grasp the true nature (to say nothing of the functioning) of the Canadian system of government.

Like most people, I've never actually worked in government. I am, always have been and will surely remain on the outside looking in. I don't know how it feels to be voted into office. I have no clue what it means to be a Cabinet minister. And I am not sure exactly what bureaucrats do.

I am not interested in running for office, and the doors of public service seem rather hermetically closed to me. Yet I still wish I had a better understanding of what those people elected to manage a fairly big part of *my* life are doing. It makes sense to study the way I am being governed, what with having to foot the bill and all.

An American intellectual who wrote a very interesting book after spending 10 years in Canada made a good point: "The shock of knowing how their country is really run would, it is assumed, be too great for Canadians to bear; and they, themselves, avert their eyes when the authorities tell them to."[1]

How can this be?

Since it is present in just about every aspect of our lives, we all want the best possible government — even if we can't seem to agree on what, exactly, "best possible government" means. Yet as citizens we want to keep an eye on things and make sure that no one is allowed to take advantage of us.

Except that we don't do much about ensuring that we have this type of government. We all expect the best of our baker, dry cleaner or car mechanic, and we make sure we hold these people accountable for whatever it is they do for us. But when it comes to government, our standards inevitably fall to levels that barely register on politicians' radar screens.

It seems as though we have somehow given up. Maybe we think governments are so big and complicated that there is nothing we can do to change things for the better, even though there are many issues that Canadians are concerned about: federal-provincial relations, health care, contaminated water, the almighty power of the Prime Minister's Office (PMO), the arrogance of some politicians, duties of the governor general, proportional representation, campaign finance, fixed election dates and so on.

Indeed, understanding our national institutions of governance is a huge task. Often we throw up our hands and say, "What do you expect? It's government. It's not supposed to make sense." Yet because we're all affected by government, and because we're the ones paying for it, most of us wish we could better understand what our leaders on the Hill are doing.

"Sure," you might think, "but how do you suggest we go about understanding and changing government?"

Good question. Very good question. After all, many people have tried, and failed — they got tired and gave up, or surreptitiously became part of the very system they wanted to change.

So what can we do?

Well, my colleagues and I decided to look at government from a rather unusual perspective — we studied its blood and guts.

"Honey, I looked into a sewer line."

Imagine coming home on a crisp autumn night and announcing, "Honey, guess what? I finally understand how government really works!"

This statement is sure to elicit a genuinely admiring response from your significant other: "Wow, how did you do *that*?"

Your response: "Oh, I looked into a sewer line." That's right, a sewer line. Not to mention leaking water mains, pothole-ridden roads and collapsing bridges. That's how we've investigated government. From the ground up. And it worked ... sort of.

This street-level research helped us understand many things about the way we Canadians govern ourselves. Much more, in fact, than if we had decided to go down the usual road — sitting in a classroom or a library, trying to absorb essentially vague information.

Surprised? Well, we were too.

Canadians have much in common: we love to criticize politicians, government and politics. We hate paying taxes. We become frustrated with government regulations. We lose our patience (and sometimes our sanity) dealing with bureaucrats. We're bored silly by political speeches and electoral campaigns.

And yet we all expect to receive what we think is our fair share of government-provided services — subsidized education, family allowances, subsidies for our firm or professional association, old age pensions, employment insurance and so on.

Every now and again we get really mad, like when there is a scandal or something. A story about government waste finds its way onto the front page of our favourite newspaper and, oh, do we ever get angry. But come election day, we usually vote the same people back into office. Whether it's the same party or new faces, nothing changes. As Patrick Boyer, an experienced political observer, likes to say, "It doesn't matter which party you vote for in an election, the government always gets in."

Yes, there is something wrong with the way we Canadians govern ourselves. You know it, I know it and the politicians probably know it as well. "Whatever, you know. Politicians are all the same anyway. Today there's a crisis; tomorrow it'll be yesterday's news."

Not an excessively deep sentiment perhaps, but quite strongly felt and fairly representative of the general mood among many folks my age. For a significant portion of the youngish generation, there is one short answer to all these political squabbles adorning every other newspaper column: "Government sucks." Period.

And many feel it's an old boys' club we're talking about — I mean, there are some women in government, but it's essentially a members only club: you're either in or you're out. The people who are in run the show, even though we on the outside have to pay the bills.

It's hard not to be cynical. After all, we've just started making a life for ourselves, just started earning a living that allows us to plan beyond the next jar of peanut butter. But we're faced with the probability that more and more money will be taken out of our pockets and used for governmental purposes that we often don't even understand.

Most people shrug the whole thing off. They have lives to live and jobs to do, and they're not terribly interested in trying to influence their system of governance. Maybe they think our national governing institutions are not worth spending much time on. It's not like you alone could make a difference anyway. So why bother, eh?

You may think this all sounds rather hopeless. But some of us refuse to avert our eyes when the authorities tell us, "We know best, trust us." We demand and expect accountability and responsibility from the people we elect to represent us. We get involved because of two things we hold dear: our future as individuals and the future of a country we care about. We think citizens have a duty to make informed choices and decisions and that elected representatives have an obligation to be reasonably accountable to those who elect them.

Sean Moore, an Ottawa-based lobbyist and columnist with *The Hill Times*, once said that if Canadians want to influence public policy, they really have to take it upon themselves to learn about how their government operates. So we decided to do just that.

Introduction

The story you're about to read began in 1994 when a group of young Canadian researchers set out to investigate the problems and people that contributed to our country's massive national debt. During the researchers' interviews (recorded for what would become a three-hour television program entitled *Days of Reckoning*) political veterans confided that even they could not understand the business of public spending. They also revealed that it is virtually impossible to track a tax dollar from the moment it is raised to the moment it is spent.

One of the researchers, Jay Innes, started investigating one specific program to test whether he could understand how government spends public money in Canada. Jay focused on the 1993 Canada Infrastructure Works Program (CIWP) — a national, $8.3-billion, tripartite government plan to repair the country's crumbling infrastructure. He chose CIWP because the details of the program were easy to explain to a large audience and because all three levels of government (federal, provincial and municipal) simultaneously implemented the program across Canada.

In the summer of 1998 Jay hired a new team of researchers, from Vancouver to Charlottetown. Their task was to find out how the infrastructure program had been implemented in their respective provinces: How had particular decisions been made — to fund project X instead of project Y — and why?

Before joining Toronto-based Stornoway Productions I had managed to earn a law degree from Laval University in Quebec City. I turned down a job in a law firm because I thought it would be more fun to make ends meet as an underpaid writer (it is). I was working as a columnist for a Montreal-based Webzine, freelancing here and there, and writing what would become, a year later, my first book. Jay Innes entered my life for what was supposed to be a summer job — a six- to eight-week research project on a government job-creation program.

I was hired as a researcher for a documentary on the Canada Infrastructure Works Program. I would be looking at roads and sewers in my home province of Quebec and gathering empirical evidence documenting how the decisions to fund particular projects had been made. The idea was to try and track a tax dollar through one spending program. Could we measure accountability by assessing whether the government was doing what it had said it would do with citizens' money?

I was a tad apprehensive about the whole thing. I had the feeling I was not quite prepared for the job. Oh sure, I thought I understood a thing or two about our system of government; I had studied constitutional law pretty intensely, and I had kept on reading about politics and current events. But I was about to discover a world in which all the premises I was used to didn't hold true. What a life lesson! I was about to learn how our system of government *really* works.

And they actually paid me for that?

Well, yes. They hired me and a bunch of other people from all across the country. In Montreal I had a teammate, a rather colourful chap named Philippe Forest. Filmmaker, writer and playwright, Philippe was straightforward, open-minded and fun. Then there was Jennifer Nunn from Charlottetown. Jenn was an experienced journalist who knew the East Coast inside out. In Toronto there was Geoff Scales, formerly with an important Crown corporation.

Anette Mueller from Winnipeg was another straightforward and open-minded character on our team. Then there was Lydia Miljan in Calgary, juggling three kids and a job while completing her Ph.D. in political science at the University of Calgary. And finally, we had Leanne Hazon in Vancouver. Leanne had just finished her degree in journalism at Carleton University in Ottawa. She was the youngest in the group, her wide-eyed tenacity more than compensating for her relative lack of experience.

The team would work under the direction of Jay Innes, based in Ottawa.

Now that we're all properly introduced, let's get back to the story. As I was saying, the idea was to track a tax dollar through one spending program to see if we could measure accountability by assessing whether the government was doing what it had said it would do with citizens' money.

To many Canadians accountability in government may sound like a contradiction in terms. Many people feel that governments are not accountable to the taxpayers; in fact, it seems that scandals abound. Sometimes millions or even billions of public dollars go missing, yet heads rarely roll down Parliament Hill. Canadians, especially the younger generations, see the future compromised by a $555-billion debt for which no one appears to take responsibility. It seems that young

Canadians are being asked to pay for someone else's unbridled spending — and are expected to do so without protest.

Look at it from our point of view: we see politicians hand out tax dollars, in the form of subsidies, to companies that frequently go belly-up. We see money earned by young families in one part of the country somehow finding its way to another part of the country to finance job-creation programs — programs that, coincidentally, last long enough to qualify the workers who benefit for another season of employment insurance. Public pension funds, we suspect, are unlikely to be sufficient for our generation to collect a penny; yet we can expect our contributions to increase sharply in order to compensate those now retiring from the workforce. Same with health care: by the time we begin experiencing health problems the system may well have collapsed.

Are we right to see things this way? Or are we being incredibly ungrateful to our parents' and grandparents' generations who built our peaceful and caring society? Does the future look so bleak to young Canadians that they'll be prompted to pack the proverbial U-Haul and leave the country in search of better opportunities?

The truth is we don't know with certainty whether we are right to see things in this way. We don't know whether the future will turn out to be as bad as we imagine because we are not encouraged to understand and question the way our politicians and bureaucrats govern our lives.

What we do know is that too many mistakes go unchecked, often at great cost to taxpayers, and that the source of our problems can be traced to a lack of accountability in government.

Accountability in government is crucial to the survival of any democratic system. We cannot afford an endless series of mistakes and scandals, believing in a happy-go-lucky Panglossian view that it's all for the best in this best of all possible worlds. Blind optimism can temporarily make people feel good, but it does not make problems go away.

Accountability means being bound to account for one's actions and having to face the consequences of those actions. Accountability in government means that those who have the power to raise and spend public money are responsible to the citizens for the way they use that money.

We think our future in Canada would look much better if we could restore accountability and responsibility in government — if we, the citizens, could regain at least some control over public spending. But

15

before we can do that we have to understand how, exactly, the Canadian system of government works.

Lack of accountability coupled with the secrecy in government (the fact that we are discouraged from questioning our governing institutions) leads to apathy, which in turn leads to even less accountability and even more secrecy. When citizens become apathetic they tend to forego asking harsh questions of the folks they elect (questions such as how, for whom, why and, more importantly, how much is all this going to cost?). And what happens then? As one former deputy minister put it, "If nobody cares, who cares?"

We want to break this vicious circle. Easier said than done.

Down the Road Never Travelled tells the story of our quest for answers to a very simple question: how did politicians and bureaucrats handle the infrastructure program? We took the road less travelled in that instead of going directly to senior policy advisors, veteran political commentators, professional lobbyists or academics, we focused our investigation on ground-level decision-making institutions. We started by trying to find answers to simple questions about specific infrastructure projects from mayors and municipal bureaucrats before moving up to higher levels of government.

Taking the road less travelled is sometimes hard. Maybe the reason is that when you travel down unusual roads, you often end up in funny places. We were asked to make a few phone calls to municipalities near where we lived to find out how and why specific decisions had been made with respect to the infrastructure program. Simple enough, we thought. To our surprise we found ourselves storming the Parliament buildings a few months later, looking for someone who could finally answer our questions.

The most remarkable aspect of this unusual search for accountability is that we eventually had to go to Ottawa to understand how and why local authorities chose to inject funds into the renovation of a theatre in Outremont, Quebec, instead of replacing that municipality's century-old and oft-leaking wooden sewers.

Are roads and sewers so complex a matter that only some inaccessible, top-level bureaucrat in Ottawa can answer questions about them? Or is there something wrong with the way we govern ourselves when citizens have to go through so much trouble just to find out why a municipality in Prince Edward Island got bowling alleys instead of a repaired road? What has happened to the mechanisms of accountability, such as the formal division of powers and the control of the public purse by members of Parliament, that were built into the Canadian Constitution? Why is it so difficult for citizens to find out how government is spending their money?

Down the Road Never Travelled is based on actual experience, not textbooks. The quest for accountability in government as chronicled in this book represents street-level, empirical research.[2]

This long and painful quest for accountability in government is a story that stands on its own. As researchers we rushed headlong into brick walls while trying to understand how building a new community centre won out over repairing a bridge. Our experiences are a powerful illustration of the lack of accountability in the Canadian system of government.

But our story also serves as an ideal springboard for discussion. It is a great starting point for a detailed study of what happened to the mechanisms of accountability that were built into our 1867 Constitution. *Down the Road Never Travelled* is an initial step in a larger educational program; it provides its reader with an empirical exposé of how Canadian government actually works today.

NOTES

1. Edgar Z. Friedenberg, *Deference to Authority: The Case of Canada* (White Plains, New York: M.E. Sharpe, 1980) p. 51.
2. During the course of our research we conducted numerous interviews with politicians, bureaucrats and ordinary citizens who were involved with the infrastructure program. I have included excerpts from many of these conversations, as well as the interviews conducted by the *Days of Reckoning* researchers, throughout this book. All quotations for which I have not explicitly cited a source, either within the text or in an accompanying note, come from this collection of interviews. Readers interested in viewing lengthier versions of the transcripts should consult *Days of Reckoning*, edited by John

Wood, *On the Money Trail: Investigating How Government Decisions are Made* by Tim Chorney with Jay Innes and *Secrets in High Places* by Jay Innes.

PART ONE

How Frustrating Can a Summer Job Be?

1. INFRA! INFRA!

A crash course in civil engineering

As noted before, some of us have a tendency not to avert our eyes when the authorities say, "We know best, trust us."

Call us skeptics.

We demand and expect accountability and responsibility from the people we send to Parliament. We believe citizens have a duty to make informed choices and decisions, and that elected representatives have an obligation to be reasonably accountable to the citizens.

As I said, accountability means being bound to account for one's actions and having to face the consequences of those actions. Accountability in government means that those who have the power to raise and spend public money are responsible to the voters for the way they use that money (and how much of it they're using).

You are probably familiar with the "brain drain" — loads of bright, young Canadians deciding to leave their troubled country behind and seek better opportunities south of the border.[1] Well, we haven't left. We have chosen to stay and fight to improve the governing institutions of our country. We are convinced our future in Canada would look much better if we could restore accountability and responsibility in government, if we, the citizens, could regain control over public spending.

But first we have to understand how, exactly, the Canadian system of government works. In particular, we have to understand how politicians and bureaucrats currently raise and spend our tax dollars.

Hence the idea of studying the Canada Infrastructure Works Program (CIWP).

The Canada Infrastructure Works Program was a cost-shared spending program involving the federal, provincial and municipal governments.[2] It promised to rejuvenate the country's decaying infrastructure while creating jobs. The newly elected Liberal government launched the initial $6-billion program in early 1994.[3] The program was supposed to provide a quick injection of money to repair the country's crumbling roads, sewers and bridges, while instantly creating jobs to ease the national unemployment rate, which had climbed to more than 10 percent.

The program also promised to foster harmonious relations among the different levels of government. Only eight weeks after announcing the program, the federal government had negotiated and signed infrastructure agreements with all 10 provinces and both territories. In recognition of the much-needed infrastructure repairs on reserves, the federal government dedicated a portion of the money to the First Nations. All three levels of government agreed to pay a third of the project costs; in some instances the private sector was encouraged to come up with project ideas in lieu of municipal involvement.

It was supposed to work like this: municipal governments would present their applications; then the provincial governments and the federal government's regional development agencies across Canada would co-chair the management committees where final decisions were made. In provinces like B.C. and Ontario the provincial governments submitted their own projects and paid the municipal third of the costs. In some impoverished municipalities in Newfoundland and Saskatchewan, the province paid the municipal share.

Now, if you're not a bureaucrat, this may seem a bit complicated. In fact, the program worked quite well administration-wise; the high level of co-operation was widely praised and cited as an example of the way governments can and indeed should work together. Politicians contrasted the infrastructure program with the bickering associated with the doomed Meech and Charlottetown accords, or with the endless arguments that characterize federal-provincial relations.[4]

"So there was this national infrastructure program," you say. "I'm still not sure why anyone would bother to study roads and sewers?" The answer is a simple one: because we care. We care about the ability of regular citizens to get their heads around government programs. We think accountability starts right there: with citizens being able to understand where their tax dollars go, and why.

Sometimes it seems that the main reason people these days can't understand government spending is because they don't care enough to ask the tough questions. Alan Ross, a former deputy minister, put it this way: "Has anybody asked to see the financial operations of the Department of Health and Welfare or National Defence? So if nobody asked the question, nobody cares. If nobody cares, who cares?" But since we do care, we decided to do something: we tracked the flow of dollars — from the taxpayers' pockets to the government and then back to citizens in the form of renewed infrastructure.

Oddly enough, we soon realized that studying leaking pipes could lead us to understand (and eventually explain) how elected representatives in Ottawa use our tax money to manage our affairs.

First, get on the phone. Then hope someone picks up.

Jay Innes had been working for roughly 18 months researching the Infrastructure Works Program from his home in Ottawa. All this time he had been trying to get bureaucrats to first, pick up the phone when he called, and second, answer at least one little question every so often.

Ah, you think, what a cushy job! The guy gets paid to make a couple of phone calls to other people who get paid *not* to answer the phone when it rings. In reality Jay was slowly wearing himself down banging his head over and over again against the same wall. (Details of Jay's adventures will be discussed in subsequent chapters.)

After those 18 gruelling months Jay finally received the OK to hire a bunch of researchers from all over the country to help him with the workload (or possibly just so he could secretly rejoice at the thought of our going through the same misery he had experienced). After he hired us and once all the work had been done, he began to see the light again, so to speak:

> Only after we brought these researchers onboard did the individual stories of the infrastructure projects start to take shape. My enthusiasm renewed, I realized that we had embarked on a unique study of a cost-sharing program that would yield insights from all six provinces. This grassroots style of assessing an issue would ultimately allow us to identify trends and make some broad and sweeping conclusions about government accountability.

Not that our research project was a walk in the park, mind you. We uncovered lots of problems with the Infrastructure Works Program. Questionable choices of project, vague guidelines, criteria wide enough for a Mack truck, financial mismanagement: these were only a few of the sins we encountered.

Toward the end of her contract Lydia, our researcher in Alberta, remembered listening to an open-line radio show during which someone called in to say Canadian voters were stupid and deserved what they got because they never asked for accountability in government. She thought, "But I've been doing just that — asking for accountability — for two and a half months! I felt like phoning in to tell him it's not that easy. '*You* try making some phone calls to ask who made the decision for this project …'"

The worst difficulty we had was trying to get individuals, either bureaucrats or politicians, to take responsibility for the decisions they had made. Accountability means being able to say to someone, "You are responsible for that decision and I, as a citizen who helped foot the bill, disagree with it. I want to know what you have to say for yourself and, in the event that the decision you made was a mistake, I want to know what you are going to do to correct it and make sure it doesn't happen again."

This kind of accountability, as you probably know very well, rarely exists in our political world. Bureaucrats are buried under rules and procedures so thick you'd lose your mind trying to figure out the table of contents. Politicians can evade harsh questions by hiding behind the rule books of bureaucracy. And everyone blames everyone else for whatever mismanagement *might* possibly have occurred. Often politicians refuse to stand before critics and answer questions, while bureaucrats move cautiously between their various sets of procedures. As a result, accountability gets squeezed out of government programs, replaced with caution and fear that work to remove the public from public service.

Understanding the basics

Studying something as basic as the state of our country's water mains, sewer lines or the roads on which we drive made us wonder what else was going on at the higher levels of government policy. Studying the basics is a great way to evaluate the performance of those in charge. If our politicians and bureaucrats don't get the small things right, how can they take care of the big things?

Infrastructure plays a vital role in any society. But what exactly does "infrastructure" mean? Experts such as Saeed Mirza, professor of civil engineering at McGill University (who is just as crazy about infrastructure as I am about Italian-roast coffee beans), explained:

> A political scientist might define "infrastructure" much more broadly than I would. But to me infrastructure would be everything that makes us live happily, efficiently and comfortably — roads, water supply, sewage systems and communications systems. You could distinguish the difference between the hard infrastructure that I just described and perhaps soft infrastructure — places like skating rinks, libraries in cities, etc. So I think that is the only distinction I would make, but I think hard infrastructure is the one that defines the quality of life for all of us.

Hard infrastructure, such as roads, bridges, sewers, water mains, filtration systems and so on — things that in the good old days were called "public works" — defines our quality of life at a rather basic level. It helps us distinguish developed nations from developing ones. In the absence of decent infrastructure some countries can hardly prosper.

Canada is part of the developed world. Canadians are a rather lucky lot. We enjoy all the modern benefits of an infrastructure-rich civilization. Turning on the tap is just about all we have to do to get clean water. We suddenly feel like going from Ottawa to Gaspé? (You should if you haven't done it yet; la Gaspésie is quite nice.) Easy, we just hop in the car and drive there.

Yet with all the modern infrastructure we have here, Canada is not doing so well. The problem, you see, is that we don't see the problem. What with being rich and modern and all, we tend to neglect what we have. As it turns out, Canadians have for many decades put off maintenance work on their roads, sewers and water-treatment plants. We have neglected to maintain our bridges. We have allowed our infrastructure to deteriorate.[5]

What happened was that during the post-war years, when everyone was doing quite fine thank you, the trend was building. Construction was *in*, and cranes and bulldozers were all over the place. "Men at work" was the motto; "Build it and they will come" were the ultimate *mots justes.*

Since everyone was busy building, nobody paid much attention to maintenance. After all, it's much more fun to be out there paving new roads than down in the trenches doing indispensable work making sure the water mains are still holding on, right? As Ron Hayter, former president of the Federation of Canadian Municipalities, put it:

> This is an ongoing problem in this country, as it is in most nations. You've got to keep on top of your infrastructure. What happened in Canada is that we got behind — drastically behind — to the point where bridges were closed, roads were pocked with potholes and underground systems were breaking up all the time.

Only a few people took the time to study and care about infrastructure maintenance. Some civil engineers — those who were not busy designing new bridges — have been compiling data on the aging of the existing infrastructure and the potential costs of delaying maintenance work any longer. And it ain't pretty.

Did you know our national infrastructure was in a really bad state? I didn't. Sure, I knew many things needed repair — after all, we folks in Montreal do know a thing or two about potholes. But I had no idea the infrastructure was crumbling so badly as to require an $8.3-billion program.

We learned some disquieting news as we conducted our research. We interviewed several engineers and mayors, as well as public works officials. We visited scary bridges and read extensively about water treatment and other such topics.

Was the state of our basic infrastructure as bad as many of the experts we met claimed it was? Or do Canadians simply like antiques? Ms. Jacqueline Clermont-Lasnier, a former municipal councillor in the affluent town of Outremont on the island of Montreal,[6] told us about the really, *really* old stuff they've got over there: "We have sewer pipes that were put in place at the turn of the century, right here in Outremont. We have sewers made of bricks and wood that threaten to crumble at any moment."

Wait a minute: Did she say some sewers were 100 years old? Here, in Canada, which is supposed to be a "young" country? Startled, I decided to research this rather disturbing piece of news a bit further. Could it be one isolated case of hygienic anachronism?

I called the public works people at the City of Montreal: "Someone in Outremont told me they have century-old sewers. Don't tell me theirs is *not* an isolated case ..."

The official, cool as a cucumber, explained to me that indeed there are *several* places in the very City of Montreal where the sewers are still made of wood, bricks and even, get a load of this, *lead*.

Lead! I thought this stuff was poisonous! "What happens if there is a leak somewhere? Are city residents simply to shrug off any threat of contamination just because the pipes are underground and they can pretend they don't see them?"

I am not sure I remember what the official's answer was to my question about the risk of contamination; but I do know "We are currently replacing all those old, dangerous pipes" was not part of it.

Upon recovering my senses I asked my fellow researchers in other provinces to inquire as to whether they also had old and dangerous sewers in their respective necks of the woods. Guess what? Almost all of them said, "Yes, we also have some old — some *very* old (i.e., turn-of-the-century) — sewers around here."

Broadcasting live from the sewer and other infrastructure stories

Winnipeg, like many other cities across Canada, has what engineers call "combined sewer systems." These systems deal with both land drainage and wastewater, and everything goes through the same pipes.

So guess what happens during heavy rainfalls. That's right: sewers back up.

Winnipeg also has sewer pipes that date back to the 1890s. Apparently those old pipes often are only kept together by the so-called Manitoba gumbo. (No, you can't eat it. It's the local variety of clay.)

To their credit, public works people in that city are doing something about the state of their infrastructure. Diane Sacher, support services engineer, explained:

> The current state of the sewers is not something that we're aware of completely in Winnipeg right now ... we've started a condition assessment program so we're televising what we've called "critical sewers" in Winnipeg, which comprise about 20 percent of the system. And throughout that television program we are determining the condition of the sewer system. Past practice is for the sewer system to be maintained, but normal condition assessment and maintenance would only occur on a reactive basis. So if there were customer complaints, then there would be some maintenance activity that would be done.

Their television program seemed to be working: at the time of her interview Ms. Sacher told Anette leaks from water mains were down to about 700 a year, from a high of about 2,100.

British Columbia had the biggest infrastructure project in the country, the Annacis water-treatment plant. (This project was big enough to attract Prime Minister Jean Chrétien to the official opening.) The plant now provides secondary treatment for close to half the wastewater that would otherwise be discharged into the Fraser River. What is important to remember here is that before this plant was built only about 60 percent of the used water was filtered before being discharged into the river. With secondary treatment almost 90 percent of the water gets treated before it goes into the Fraser River, which is both an important breeding ground for waterfowl and home to 85 species of fish.

Surely, you think, these stories of sewage water getting dumped in rivers only happen in remote areas or in small towns where there is not enough money to address pressing infrastructure needs. None of this could ever happen in a place like Toronto, right?

Well, actually, it could happen in Toronto. One reason why the beaches there were closed to swimming and bathing during the summer was a one-pipe system that carried both sanitary flow and storm water. When it rained all that stuff would overflow into the lake, polluting the water and the beaches. Last time we talked to him, Toronto's director of engineering, Warner Wickman, was busy putting up some kind of storm sewer to hold the water while the sewer system dealt with the overflow.[7]

In Langley, British Columbia, city officials needed money to build an overpass because the trains that ran through Langley could cut off the entrance and exit to the city, causing a traffic buildup. More importantly, the overpass would allow emergency response teams to get through. Once, a man whose scalp was on fire had to be pulled from his vehicle by another person on the other side of the train, who had to climb through the boxcars to get to him because emergency vehicles couldn't get through.[8]

In Montreal there was an old abandoned bridge east of Olympic Stadium. Built in 1960, this 400-metre-long structure had deteriorated so badly the authorities had to close it to traffic in 1993.

The list goes on.

When citizens fail to ask for maintenance

Are our politicians willing to let the existing infrastructure collapse while they're spending our money on golf courses or new community centres? The answer, apparently, is yes. When citizens are not concerned about something, politicians are not concerned with it either. And when politicians are not concerned about something, they obviously don't spend money on it. That is why infrastructure deteriorated: because citizens failed to ask politicians to spend money on maintenance. Politicians spend money on stuff the electorate wants. No demand, no money. No money, no infrastructure maintenance.

Winnipeg engineer Diane Sacher explained:

What we find is that the public in the past has focused on water main leaks when they're occurring. We get a lot of calls from the public about sewer repairs in particular if [the sewers] are affecting the pavement. The problem is no longer underground;

29

it's affecting the citizens' day-to-day lives and they're concerned about it.

As it turns out, in Winnipeg it was mostly engineers, academics and a couple of bureaucrats who called for infrastructure maintenance — and you know how easily both citizens and politicians can ignore these people.

In an article published in the *Winnipeg Free Press* on September 18, 1991, John Redfern, chairman of the Coalition to Renew Canada's Infrastructure (CRCI) said:

> The problem in a nutshell is that governments at all levels are not spending enough funds to maintain roads, bridges, sewers and water mains at their designed levels of efficiency and reliability. As a result, Canadians are wasting fuel, time and money, endangering their health and environment and, in the process, becoming less competitive in the new global economy.[9]

That same newspaper article reported the results of a study group established two years earlier by the council of ministers responsible for transportation and highway safety. The study had found that 38 percent of highway networks deemed to be of national importance were substandard, and that 22 percent of the bridges on that system required major strengthening or rehabilitation. The 25,000-kilometre national highway system accounts for only three percent of the total road network, but carries nearly 26 percent of all vehicle traffic.

As an indication of how little municipalities spend on infrastructure maintenance, let's consider the example of Outremont. Former councillor Clermont-Lasnier explained to us that it spends on average five percent of its money on infrastructure. Because citizens usually don't demand improvements to infrastructure, municipal authorities tend to "defer" maintenance work.

As Professor Mirza explained to us, this inadequate funding leads to an infrastructure deficit: an infrastructure deficit is the difference between the money needed to improve the infrastructure and bring it to an acceptable level and the money earmarked for infrastructure and maintenance. In 1985 Professor Mirza told us the

Canadian infrastructure deficit was $12 billion. In 1993 it had ballooned to $44 billion.

Why tolerate such a deficit? Because governments (and sometimes private organizations as well) only think about what kind of investment would be needed to build an infrastructure facility like a bridge or a water supply system, without giving much thought to what will happen later on. How will this bridge, road, etc., be maintained? Ten years from now, 15 years from now, will there be any need for major rehabilitation?

From what we could discover many people don't seem to care enough about prevention and maintenance of infrastructure. Instead, we wait until roads or bridges get to a point where it's dangerous to drive on them and then close them for two months for major repairs.[10] And it's even worse underground: when big problems do occur, everyone seems surprised at how much the replacement of a pipe will cost.

This is a silly way to take care of business. Infrastructure maintenance should be like going to the dentist. Most of us don't wait until we have an unbearable toothache; we go regularly, and we carefully floss and brush our teeth. Because we constantly pay attention to our natural teeth, we get to keep them. In the end it costs us less and we're better off than if we had had to put up with dentures.

Why don't we do the same with public works? Unfortunately, most politicians don't want to "waste" their time on underground stuff. Few people are interested in going to the opening of a new sewer line. Politicians are not likely to enjoy boasting about the waterworks maintenance schedule in the glossy newsletters they send their constituents. As a result, water supply and sewage disposal systems get the least attention; in several provinces the pipes are so deteriorated and perforated that about 35 to 50 percent of clean water is being lost. When the pipes are perforated, there is no way to know what is coming into them and contaminating the water everybody drinks.

When do people realize an underground problem is in fact a problem? Or does it take a tragedy such as the E. coli outbreak in Walkerton, Ontario? In May 2000 the bacterium infected the small town's water system, killing seven people and sending dozens of others to the hospital with severe cramps and other terrible symptoms.

The problem, you see, is that we don't see the problem.

As noted, the problem with infrastructure management is that we often don't see the problem. Diane Sacher explained:

> It is very easy to put a pipe in the ground and say that pipe has a 50-year life. It's underground; it's providing the service and we don't have to worry about it until there's a problem. When the pipes are underground and they're functioning well, they don't get much attention from the public.

As far as I can understand it, infrastructure maintenance in Canada works like this: someone puts a pipe down, and then everybody proceeds to forget about it until one day someone else drives into a pothole big enough to swallow Ms. Palmer's kids.[11]

Canadian municipalities, it seems, manage their infrastructure according to how angry their citizens get by driving into the same bloody pothole every single day. Do engineers and public works employees fix a sewer problem only if the public has given attention to it? Sewer pipes need frequent maintenance, one would assume, but who makes sure this maintenance work is taken care of?

We asked Professor Mirza, who explained:

> When the city's facility department or the infrastructure department goes to the municipal council to ask for money and says, "Look, we have to renovate this road this year," the first question the council asks is, "Can it wait until next year?" And, you know, the engineers think about it and I guess they arrive at a consensus after some discussion that, yes, it can wait. It waits one year; it waits a second year; it waits a third year. And finally, in five or six years, the road has deteriorated to such an extent that the municipality ends up spending five times or 10 times the money it would have spent initially. So basically this is like cancer. Once deterioration sets in it grows at a very rapid rate.

The most frustrating thing in all this for us was that nobody seemed too concerned about "opportunity costs" — the idea that if you spend a dollar on one thing, you can't spend it on another thing. So when you decide to spend your dollar on that one thing, not only do you have to think about whether or not that thing is worth spending your dollar on, you also have to ask yourself whether it's more worthwhile than spending that dollar on something else.

Anette asked Milton Boyd, an economist with the University of Manitoba, whether he thought public authorities in Canada think about opportunity costs when they make their decisions. His response:

> I think the government faces the same question that we do as families or individuals. We have a dollar and what are we going to do with that dollar? Are we going to invest it so that in 30 years we have something to show for that dollar? Or are we going to consume it now and enjoy the short-term pleasure of that dollar? Now, as individuals we strike a balance and each of us strikes that balance differently. But when it comes to the government, it has an obligation to future generations. If it takes a dollar today and spends that public dollar, the future generations have only a debt for that dollar it borrowed. It has consumed everything. On the other hand, if the government spends that money on investments, then future generations have a bridge that they need, they have a building that they need ... it's a long-term investment rather than short-term consumption.

In other words, when citizens put pressure on politicians to build a new recreation centre without wondering about whether it would be better to spend that money on much-needed basic repairs to their town's core infrastructure, long-term investments such as bridges or sewer systems deteriorate and everybody is worse off. As Professor Boyd added, "My generation spends a dollar today and to spend that dollar it has to borrow it. Then the next generation has to pay back the debt. And so today, if I haven't spent that dollar wisely ... I've done a disservice to future generations."

Imagine if we took the same approach to home repairs: "Honey, the roof is leaking in Little Johnny's bedroom. And then there's the garage door squeaking all the time. One day the bearings are going to be so rusted out that the whole thing may collapse."

"Yeah, sure. But can it wait until next year? There's this neat DVD player I really want to get."

It wouldn't work because if you waited a year, then poor Little Johnny would be swimming all night long and you wouldn't be able to get into your garage. So you manage to put off other, less urgent expenses in order to put first things first. Not because you're a genius, but because doing the repairs as soon as they're needed is the best thing to do.

Unless, that is, your strategy is to let your house crumble while you watch Bruce Willis blowing stuff up on a giant TV screen.

What I can't see can't bother me, right?

With your teeth or your house, it is rather easy to plan your infrastructure repair. You know your house; you live in it. You are the one who will benefit from smart decisions or pay the consequences for bad ones. But when you're dealing with a country as large as Canada, things are a bit more complicated. Decisions made in Alberta don't affect the folks in Gaspé too much. And too often the consequences of bad decisions are left for subsequent generations to deal with. That's why it is important that there be someone, somewhere, with an eye on the big picture. You want people planning repairs, maintenance work, new construction, etc. And you want their advice when it's time to decide how much public money is going to go where.

Among other things, this type of infrastructure planning and decision making is what the Federation of Canadian Municipalities (FCM) is there for.

At the beginning of my investigation in the province of Quebec, I kept coming across accounts of how the FCM had pushed and pulled relentlessly for over 15 years to get politicians at the federal and provincial levels to get involved in a nationwide infrastructure-renewal program.

What exactly is the FCM, and who does it represent? I wondered.

So I asked Jay, who always seems to know the answers to these questions. "It represents more than 600 municipalities across the country," he explained, "and carries considerable lobbying strength in the corridors of power. It is well connected to MPs who moved to federal politics after cutting their teeth at the municipal level. Its power was strengthened in the spring of 1998 when Ontario MP Bryon Wilfert, a former president of the FCM, formed a municipal caucus within the federal government."

So influential is the FCM that, according to *National Post* columnist Paul Wells, almost every item in the chapter on municipal affairs in the Liberal 2000 campaign platform responded to a demand from the FCM:

> When the Federation of Canadian Municipalities meets, twice a year, the power elite come running. Mr. Chrétien never misses the annual conference in the spring. He usually brings a half dozen ministers with him. Last year every other party leader showed up too. Even Gilles Duceppe. The FCM's crowning demonstration of political clout was the first "infrastructure" program, $6-billion worth of sewers, sportsplexes and community halls, a centrepiece of Mr. Chrétien's 1993 campaign. Since then, despite serious questions about the wisdom of make-work on such a massive scale, the feds have implemented Infrastructure II and in the last election promised Infrastructure III.[12]

The idea here is that we have to keep our eyes on the ball, as it were, and on decision makers. And we have to pay special attention to accountability. We want to monitor closely those people we have elected to manage our tax dollars and who are responsible for making decisions as to what kind of services are to be delivered with how much money.

Most of the problems we found with the infrastructure program resulted from the difference between the 1980s concept of the program and what the new Liberal federal government delivered in 1994. As former FCM president Ron Hayter, who had been on Edmonton city council for 24 years and is now retired, explained:

> It was the FCM that really initiated the idea of a national infrastructure program. The idea goes back to 1986 when it was obvious to municipal members that the infrastructure across this country, the basic infrastructure, streets and roads and bridges, was in need of repair. The program that was devised at that time was called The "Big Fix." Unfortunately, we weren't able to get the support of provincial governments or the federal government of the day. As a result, that particular program didn't make much headway.

Mr. Hayter said the reason why it took so long to get government to agree to participate in the FCM proposal for an infrastructure program was that the proposal "concentrated on the basic infrastructure, roads, streets, bridges, and that stuff isn't very sexy. And most of it's underground where people don't see it. So you can tell them there's a problem but a lot of people don't know it's a problem, don't realize there is a problem because they can't see it." So what the FCM had to do was to change its approach to make it more interesting to vote-hungry politicians.

The FCM, according to Mr. Hayter, started working on a three-pronged approach, emphasizing the importance of repairing crumbling infrastructure, creating jobs and attracting industry and business to communities. This approach, Mr. Hayter said, was much more appealing to politicians. Unfortunately, as we'll see in Chapter 2, appealing to politicians may not always be the best strategy.

The original 1986 Big Fix was partly based on a report published by McGill University — a report that warned against letting an already crumbling infrastructure deteriorate any further. The report said that failure to act would mean that major cities would continue to pollute the waterways, and that dilapidated roads would scare potential investors and frighten tourists away from visiting Canada. Also, the report pointed out that the repair costs would only continue to increase if we put off the inevitable.

In the early 1980s the bill for the necessary repairs was $15 billion. At that time John Turner was the leader of the federal Liberals. His party endorsed the Big Fix and committed to implementing the program.

In 1987 opposition parties started attacking the governing Tories for ignoring the serious problems with the national infrastructure. The Liberals justified this intrusion into provincial jurisdiction (according to the Constitution, roads and sewers, like pretty much every other "local" matter, are a matter of provincial jurisdiction) on the basis that water and sewer problems were really pollution problems, an area which falls under federal jurisdiction.[13]

The Liberals entered the 1988 election claiming that if these pollution problems were not addressed, the cost to solve them would compound. They lost the election. After John Turner's departure in the early 1990s the new leader of the Liberal party, Jean Chrétien, adopted the Big Fix infrastructure platform. At the time of the 1993 federal election the

FCM presented an updated estimate of the cost for repairing Canada's infrastructure. It was then $44 billion.

The Liberals won the 1993 election and implemented a $6-billion program that was supposed to last two years (costs would be shared equally between the federal, provincial and municipal governments). The program ended up funding more than 17,000 projects at a cost of $8.3 billion over almost six years.

Charlie Campbell, former P.E.I. deputy minister for intergovernmental affairs, recalled:

> When the new federal government was elected in 1993, the Liberals wanted to quickly establish themselves and announced an infrastructure program that was kind of fast-tracked. They set up a special implementation task force in Ottawa under the Honourable Art Eggleton, who was a former mayor of Toronto. They had the draft agreements ready rather quickly, which they then sent out to the provinces to react to. So, in fact this series of events does prove that when the federal government wants things to happen, they can happen.

Art Eggleton was a prime player in the Federation of Canadian Municipalities and had a hand in shaping the infrastructure proposal of the 1980s when he was mayor of Toronto. It was in large part because of his FCM background that he was handed the file as president of the Treasury Board and the minister in charge of infrastructure. The Treasury Board is responsible for writing government cheques and had the final say on administering the program.[14]

Tell me what you're going to do …

One of the first steps in achieving accountability in government is having a clear declaration of intent. We elect politicians partly because of promises they make, and we judge their performance according to whether or not they keep those promises. In the particular case of the Canada Infrastructure Works Program, the two main promises were to repair our crumbling infrastructure and to create jobs.

The Liberal government was elected in 1993 partly because of its promise to create jobs. Unemployment rates in the early 1990s were awfully high, and pretty much everyone in Canada was desperate to see government doing something — *anything* — about it.

As Art Eggleton said to the House of Commons:

> The program will have a substantive impact on unemployment. In fact, the Federation of Canadian Municipalities has estimated that for every billion dollars invested, some 20,000 jobs are created ... the infrastructure program is an integral part of the vision of the new Liberal government to lay the foundation for economic recovery, to kick-start a sluggish economy and provide a future for Canadians.[15]

Many of those who were critical of the CIWP simply objected to the way the national infrastructure program was set up and implemented. For instance, several critics denounced the fact that the infrastructure program had focused too much on so-called "sexy" projects — such as community centres or soccer fields — as opposed to spending much-needed money on repairs to the nation's crumbling roads and sewers.

The important thing to remember is this: accountability needs clear definitions and clear intentions. The government wouldn't dream of implementing a $6-billion program on such an imprecise basis. Or would it?

NOTES

1. For more information, see Stornoway's one-hour television show on the "brain drain," which aired on Global Television in November 1999.
2. Cost-shared program: a program in which two or more levels of government share the costs.
3. Costs would eventually reach a little over $8.3 billion for a program that lasted almost six years.
4. This newly found "efficient federalism" will be discussed in greater detail in Chapter 3.

5. The state of core infrastructure throughout Canada is something about which politicians, bureaucrats, engineers and academics argue all the time. This is a big country, and there's almost no way one could come up with an exhaustive review of all the infrastructure currently in place. Our main focus was decision-making processes within government. For those interested in the technical and/or academic literature on core infrastructure throughout the country, the Federation of Canadian Municipalities at www.fcm.ca is a good place to start.

6. As of January 1, 2002, Outremont is a "neighbourhood" of Montreal, rather than a "town".

7. Mr. Wickman used the expression "retention tanks."

8. As necessary as the Langley overpass may seem, city officials did not get money from the CIWP for this particular project.

9. Bud Robertson, "New group bids to stop decay," *Winnipeg Free Press,* September 18, 1991, p. 19.

10. For example, commuters in the Montreal area periodically have to make do with a missing bridge between the island and the surrounding suburbs.

11. This statement is a generalization and there may be exceptions to it. But in our extended research across the country, we didn't see any.

12. Paul Wells, "Caucus a quiet show of political clout," *National Post,* February 26, 2001, p. A2.

13. Constitutional jurisdiction will be discussed in Chapter 3.

14. The Treasury Board is the manager of the government's spending, hiring, collective bargaining, bilingualism programs, administrative activities and all personal policies in the public service.

15. Canada, Parliament, *Debates,* Vol. 133, no. 5 (January 21, 1994) p. 138.

2. THE STRETCHING OF THE WORD

How we discovered that in politics people do not necessarily mean what they say

The government implemented a national infrastructure program in 1993 to repair the country's crumbling infrastructure while creating jobs. In the official documentation as well as in reports from the auditors general who studied the program afterward, infrastructure refers to "any physical capital assets in Canada instrumental in the provision of public services."

One of the first questions cynics ask when they hear about government programs is this: how do we know the government is really going to use the money the way it said it would? Not do something else, not *anything* else. Simply and plainly, that it will do what it said it would.

Fair enough. After all, this business of governments using public money for something other than that for which it was collected is not exactly new. One of the ways governments appear ridiculous is by introducing spending programs that end up doing something completely different from their original purposes. (For instance, the government initiates a job-creation program and then turns around and uses the money to finance a water fountain.)

How is it that governments can get away with spending public money in ways other than those for which it was raised? One reason is that government spending programs are often drafted in imprecise ways that allow politicians to stretch the programs in all sorts of directions. Such imprecision poses a big problem for accountability.

What is important to remember for now is this: if we, the citizens, are to hold our governments to account, we need those governments to spell out their intentions clearly — exactly how are they going to use citizens' money? Accountability needs predictability.

Accountability is not about whether projects are worthy or good. Rather, it's about respecting the rules and conditions as they appear in the political platforms or spending programs that have been "sold" to voters. If taxpayers agree to have their money spent repairing core infrastructure, repaired core infrastructure is what they should get.

On the importance of being politically sexy

Our first "surprise" when we started studying the Canada Infrastructure Works Program was the discovery of an impressive number of projects that had nothing to do with basic infrastructure. Money went to finance such projects as the Calgary Saddledome, Vancouver bike paths, bocce courts in Toronto, a Montreal tennis stadium and countless community centres across the land.

I say "surprise" because we had been warned by Jim Silye, a former Alberta MP:

> There's a big difference between legitimate funding for infrastructure, which I feel is a government responsibility, and those dubious areas where leading businesspeople or local politicians get their pet projects onto the drawing board and get them done — whether it's an arena, a hall or maybe even something named after the politician, I don't know. That's not proper infrastructure.

Mr. Silye told us that with a bit of research we'd find many similar cases across Canada. And we did: many theatres, tennis courts, golf courses and entertainment troupes received money from the infrastructure program. Did any of these projects have anything to do with repairing crumbling bridges and pothole-ridden roads? Well, no.[1]

In the province of Quebec, where I was working with Philippe, we came across a few of these questionable infrastructure projects. One was the $7.5-million renovation of an art-deco theatre in Outremont. Once renovated, the theatre was to open its doors in the spring of 1996.[2]

Councillor Jacqueline Clermont-Lasnier explained to us that this particular project had been submitted to please the general public — as opposed to quietly providing non-flashy yet important core infrastructure. The rebirth of the theatre, she said, was an electoral promise. When municipal officials learned of the infrastructure program, they hurriedly bought the crumbling building. Clermont-Lasnier recalled:

> I was in the opposition and I opposed the purchase of the Outremont Theatre and its inclusion in the infrastructure program. But I was in the minority and these choices were rather political. I figured it did not meet the infrastructure criteria. The purchase of a theatre was not, for me, going in the right direction. To my surprise the project was accepted, and you would have to ask the people concerned why they accepted the project.

The Outremont municipal council wasn't permitted to buy land with the infrastructure money. But if it could scrape together the funds to purchase the property on which the theatre sat, then the renovations would be taken care of at one-third the cost to the local government.

Tennis, anyone?

We found a few projects that made us raise our eyebrows. The world-famous Cirque du Soleil received $14 million to build a school and training centre in Montreal. Wealthy Intrawest Corp. got $10 million for the development of the Mt. Tremblant ski resort. And Tennis Canada netted $24 million for the new tennis stadium in Montreal's Jarry Park. Twenty-four million dollars on a brand-new tennis stadium (of which $20 million came from public coffers) so that Montreal could keep the Canadian Open.

"Wait a minute," you say. "Didn't anyone ask whether this spending was worthwhile?"

We thought that was a pretty good question. So we went ahead and asked Richard Legendre, at that time the Quebec director of Tennis Canada.[3] Was it worth it to spend all this public money (which, in case you forgot, was supposed to go to repairing roads and sewers) on a new tennis stadium? He told us about the difficulty of calculating the benefits of these types of projects:

> It is always difficult to arrive at a mathematical equation that will say this project is worth it. The best example representing the difficulty of assessment for us, and it is a touchy situation, is the international visibility of Montreal, Quebec and Canada. At the time people were saying we cannot afford to lose an event of this magnitude because of its international visibility. It is difficult to assess. How do you assess the value of seeing Montreal mentioned in a Japanese newspaper? It is hard to quantify.

We don't want to sound as though we're criticizing all these projects; indeed, the new Jarry Stadium is remarkable. But when voters agree to fund an infrastructure program, the money should not be spent on a new tennis centre.

Then there was this business with grand convention centres. In Quebec City politicians chose to spend over $80 million to build a new convention centre — a decision that was taken *and made public* before any agreement was signed between Quebec and Ottawa.[4]

Questionable as it was, the Quebec City convention centre was nothing compared to the jewel of the infrastructure program, the grandiose National Trade Centre in Toronto, a massive undertaking which, at $180 million, ate up most of the CIWP money allocated to Toronto and raised the ire of more than a few people.

Did Toronto really need *another* trade centre? Armies of experts and consultants fought over this particular question. We will not add to this already byzantine argument because that question is irrelevant for our purposes. We are interested in government accountability — that is, whether or not governments do what they said they would do with our money. In the case of the National Trade Centre it is painfully clear that every government involved stretched the definition of core infrastructure far enough to include the construction of a brand-new building whose necessity was widely challenged.

As Toronto councillor Jack Layton explained, the choice was between having to split the funding between a whole bunch of small initiatives (roads, transit, environment, etc.) and lose the Trade Centre, or take this opportunity to build a facility that could be a long-term economic engine for Toronto:

> It can make us a centre of ideas and ideas exchange, which is what the great cities of the world are. They are never manufacturing centres for any one particular commodity for very long. They're centres of ideas and where ideas are exchanged and developed, and the Trade Centre really fits into that long-term economic viability philosophy.

We have indeed come a long way from roads and sewers. As Mr. Layton said, projects such as the National Trade Centre were certainly not the kind of thing the Federation of Canadian Municipalities had initially been calling for. "But in retrospect," he continued, "it is a piece of urban infrastructure; it is part of what allows a city to thrive. I think the National Trade Centre was a good example of actually, in a creative and I think quite positive way, using the infrastructure program to produce spinoff benefits because now there's ongoing investment in the city as a result of that trade centre."

Sure, in retrospect (and especially now that the $180-million building is actually *there*) people line up to say how brilliant an idea it was to build it. But we were still wondering how that decision had been made beforehand, and why. We asked another councillor, Ila Bossons. She replied:

> There are two ingredients to many decisions that a councillor makes. One is facts, the other is pride or what you want your city to look like. There are probably some councillors who didn't even read the reports, who only made their decisions based on the pride factor. We wanted to put Toronto on the map with the National Trade Centre. So sometimes you didn't even have to read the documentation, or if the documentation told you it's not a good idea to build it, you might have said, "Well, they're wrong. I do believe in the future of this city. I, therefore, will vote for it." You have to remember that political decisions are not physics where one thing has to follow logically upon the other. There are emotions involved in decision making. So the facts don't always count.

In this case it looks like the pride factor won out over accountability and respect for the conditions set out in the infrastructure program.

We were not the only ones to lament the lack of accountability in the infrastructure program. Several newspaper articles criticized the funding of questionable projects. We also met quite a few people whose frustration was palpable. One of these was Dan Kelly, the Manitoba director of the Canadian Federation of Independent Business. His take on the infrastructure program is worth quoting in extenso:

> I think the federal government used the word "infrastructure" very deliberately. Infrastructure is something that Canadians generally ... feel warm and fuzzy toward. I think that the federal government, knowing that, decided to use the term infrastructure because it has that broad public policy acceptance. Whether you're on the left or right side of the equation, I think the word infrastructure is something that most people feel positively predisposed toward.
>
> Having worked with governments closely for a number of years, it is pretty clear to me that a great number of decisions are made to justify spending that is used for a variety of purposes that are beyond the original intention. I think the infrastructure program is a classic example of that. It is in many respects money that was spent to try to improve the lot of political parties and instead was justified as being so-called infrastructure money. That to me stretches the definition but it is not a surprise at all. Anyone who has been close to government knows that to make the case for spending dollars, you have to come up with a variety of rationales. In this case the rationale was the need to create jobs, the need to put some Canadians back to work, the need to improve some of our core infrastructure and perhaps the need to reduce the financial burden at our local levels in terms of property tax dollars.

Another factor that contributed to the stretching of the definition of infrastructure was multiculturalism. Dan Kelly pointed this out:

> If governments want to use infrastructure dollars to pay for multicultural programs, let's call them multicultural programs.

Let's not try to hide the word infrastructure into some spending and then use it for other purposes. You know, we elect our politicians and assume that when we elect them and choose their platform that they're going to deliver on that, not that they're going to create a whole bunch of other programs and put other more politically correct names on them and then pass them through the system that way.

In the early stages of our research we kept coming across news stories of new bocce courts that had been built in the Toronto area with infrastructure money. While the construction of such courts appeared to be a stretch of the definition of infrastructure, criticizing the use of infrastructure money for their construction was seen as some kind of minority bashing.

Toronto councillor Jack Layton:

Projects such as bocce courts are a very small investment in a small recreational facility, but typical of the media, they've decided to use it as an icon for how money was actually spent. I think that's really quite an unfair characterization of the program to do that. Number one because those projects were decided by the City of Toronto. They wanted to have a number of infrastructure improvements, and parks and recreation services are infrastructure improvements. You tell me that a playground set of swings, for example, that's rusting and falling apart shouldn't be invested in as part of maintaining a city's infrastructure? I'd say you're wrong. It's just as important a part of the city's infrastructure for the well-being of the citizens as the roads. A bocce court is a facility for seniors, primarily eastern and southern European, to play sports. [Had] we been talking about lawn bowling or golf courses or other more typically Anglo-Saxon or North American kinds of sports and making those available, I'm not sure you would have had the same reaction. Frankly, I find this reaction around the bocce courts to be pretty close to racist.

We wanted to get beyond this type of debate. We wanted to peer behind the scenes and examine the process that goes on when municipal governments make spending decisions. We found, however, that we were being attacked for merely asking the question. We would not be deterred just because someone threatened us with the word "racism." We were asking valid questions about the way money was spent on an infrastructure program.[5]

We were strengthened in our resolve by former Toronto councillor Ila Bossons:

> Of all of the cities in this country, Toronto is probably most capable of finding what it desperately needs from property tax. But there are other cities that can't even do that. There are cities in this country that don't even have safe drinking water; they have not invested in proper water filtration. That's Third World! That is not what we say is a modern country. So there are gaps in the system and it's regrettable that we have spent federal-provincial money on things like bocce courts or ice rinks when we miss some of the true basics of life in this country.

Prince Edward Island presented a similar situation, where infrastructure funds were used to subsidize the construction of bowling alleys. In Tyne Valley, P.E.I., a big chunk of CIWP money went into building a brand-new facility, the Tyne Valley Bowling Alley. We were told this is the only 10-pin bowling centre on the island — something in which the locals take pride.

But core infrastructure it ain't. Why was CIWP money spent on this bowling alley? Did P.E.I. have no problems whatsoever with its roads and sewers? According to Steven Ellis, past president of the Tyne Valley Firemen's Club (where the bowling alley is located), the spending decision had to do with the need for rural communities to provide services in order to survive:

> We have to make Tyne Valley a place where people want to live. And that's what we want to do in this community. We want to be able to provide services. We want to make it a nice place to live. And we think that's one of the strongest selling points that we could possibly have for our community.

At the other end of the country we were very busy too. As Leanne, our researcher in Vancouver, discovered, the federal government had agreed with the province of British Columbia to spend 15 percent of its $800-million infrastructure funding on "soft" infrastructure projects — that is, projects that did not include repairing crumbling roads, sewers and bridges.

Among the soft projects was the renovation of the Stanley Theatre in Vancouver, as well as many, *many* bike paths across the province.

The Stanley is a heritage movie theatre built in 1930. It closed in 1991 at a time when a lot of movie theatres of that size were closing down across the country. People interested in heritage buildings in Vancouver formed a "Save the Stanley" committee. Now they are transforming the Stanley into a live theatre.

The budget started at $6.9 million — including $3 million to buy the building — and has ballooned to over $9 million. A delay in getting the project done has certainly increased the cost. Also, it seems there has been a change of plans.

Bill Millerd, director of the Arts Club Theatre and the person in charge of the Stanley Theatre, explained that originally the project was for two theatres. "By restoring it as one theatre," he added, "it will certainly be much more glorious than it would have been. But some of the extra money went into just the efforts to really make it a very special theatre."

When we asked him what he thought of the criticism of soft projects like the Stanley, Mr. Millerd replied:

> I think it's a little shortsighted in that cultural facilities are absolutely necessary for the health and survival of a community. It's not just about roads and sewers. Of course those are vital and necessary, but public facilities like the Stanley Theatre are part of the reason why we live in a community and enjoy the community. I feel that the federal government, in insisting that 15 percent be devoted to cultural facilities, was very forward in its thinking.

Not everybody agreed. Doug McCallum, the mayor of Surrey, was very critical of the way the infrastructure program had been implemented in British Columbia. Mayor McCallum wasn't opposed to spending 15 percent on cultural projects, but as he said, "When you don't get any or very little of the transportation infrastructure, but you do get some of the cultural facilities, then it begins to appear that the priorities of the infrastructure program, at least in our region, were all wrong."

Surrey is one of the fastest growing cities in Canada. It has an urgent need for new and improved roads — businesses often have problems getting their goods into the city because their trucks are caught in gridlock. Surely the infrastructure program could have helped to alleviate this problem? Listen to Mayor McCallum:

> It was interesting in Surrey that we got some money for bike paths, which we didn't even ask for. That kind of shocked all of us. We got some money for something we didn't even ask for, and something that wasn't a priority with us. We didn't get any money for infrastructure, but all of a sudden we got some money to build bike paths.

Surrey was not the only city to receive unsolicited money for unwanted bike paths. When we met with then Richmond mayor Greg Halsey-Brandt, he told us that his municipality had received money for some bicycle-lane improvements they never requested.[6]

So what was wrong in British Columbia? Two things. The first was the 15 percent quota for cultural/soft projects; the second was that one level of government (the province) was trying to impose its own agenda on another level of government (the municipalities). We will discuss this aspect of tripartite agreements in Chapter 3.

The example of British Columbia illustrates what happens when politicians start distorting (they might call it "interpreting") the criteria of a governmental spending program. As Mayor Halsey-Brandt put it:

> The problem is that once you introduce the cultural component to it, the whole program starts to fly apart. Normally for roads, sewers or water, there's not a big public constituency out there that's lobbying for its little road or sewer. But if you introduce something like an ice arena or a theatre, there's a whole crowd that thinks a particular project should be number one on the priority list. As soon as you introduce the new project into the

formula, it has a tendency to expand and take over the whole infrastructure program. There is a lot of public demand for these sorts of highly visible facilities. That's the downside. It wasn't the original intent [of the program].

Things weren't much better in Manitoba. Our researcher Anette found that 29 community centres had received almost $1.9 million from the federal government while Winnipeg's sewer system was experiencing thousands of leaks every year. The only significant amount of money that went to core infrastructure, as far as Anette could find out, was $20 million for the installation of new separate sewers designed to avoid backups. But absolutely nothing for repairs or maintenance.

Meanwhile, in Alberta Lydia's research showed that a lot of CIWP money went to professional sports franchises. Somehow infrastructure money found its way to the Saddledome arena in Calgary and the Northlands Coliseum in Edmonton. In both cities infrastructure money was also used to fix stadiums that are home to professional baseball teams.

Funny that this kind of funding should happen, considering what Art Eggleton, Treasury Board president and minister responsible for infrastructure, had said to the Committee on Government Operations on March 16, 1994:

> We are not in the business of supporting professional sport or building luxury boxes or anything like that. If there are other aspects of those projects that have to do with economic development, we'll have a good look at them.[7]

Economic development then? The Saddledome was built in 1988 for the Winter Olympics. Its only problem was that it lacked revenue-generating private luxury boxes. Even though the Calgary Flames are a private business, they managed indirectly to secure $12-million worth of CIWP money to renovate their arena.

And just how did they do that? Well, no one really knows. It seems as though it just *happened*. Former Calgary MP Jim Silye, who represented the riding that was home to the Saddledome when the government was considering funding, told us he had not heard about the proposal, which was not on the original list submitted to the Alberta-Ottawa management committee:

> I saw a list of 20 or 30 items that had been applied for under the infrastructure program in Calgary. I did not see any Olympic Saddledome on that list. It was only after it was approved and after the deal was done that I found out about it. I had no say. At the end of the day it showed up.

According to former Calgary alderman Rick Smith, there were hundreds of projects on the list — the city had $145-million worth of infrastructure money to use over a very short period of time. The Saddledome, he said, was one of the hundreds of projects worthy of consideration.[8]

Except that this project was not about core infrastructure.

Yes, agreed Vancouver councillor George Puil, who was on the original Big Fix committee, the focus of the infrastructure program had changed:

> The original infrastructure program was at the federal level, and it was changed because of MPs who had influence, who wanted things done for their specific constituency. And the most high-profile things are not sewer projects or secondary treatment plants; they are things such as theatres, convention centres, community centres and things of that nature. [In the original program] we were quite specific as to what infrastructure meant. We gave examples of infrastructure where we felt work had to be done. So I don't think there was any confusion as far as the federal government was concerned. But the MPs soon became aware that ... they could do things that would enhance their own political position in a particular constituency, and that's how the money was used.

At this point we had enough evidence to conclude that politicians and bureaucrats all over the country had stretched the definition of infrastructure to include all sorts of flashy projects on their lists. We were not quite sure how, technically, these decisions were made; but we knew the results. Our next question was why. Why do politicians and bureaucrats behave in this way with taxpayers' money?

When we asked North York councillor John Fillion whether he thought the infrastructure program had been abused, he said:

> Well, it depends what you mean by "abused." The money was turned over to municipal politicians. Municipal politicians did what municipal politicians do, which is try to get facilities for their communities. You know, we all represent wards and geographic areas. Part of our job is to make sure that if we have an old playground, we get a new playground; if your residents are screaming for a bocce court, then you get them a bocce court; if you need a community centre, you get the community centre. So it's not like the municipal politicians did anything terribly wrong. They did exactly what municipal politicians do.

University of Ottawa professor Caroline Andrew and her co-author Jeff Morrison offered a slightly different explanation of why a program aimed at repairing Canada's crumbling infrastructure ended up funding new community centres and theatres. The problem, they said, was that the definition of infrastructure set out in the Canada Infrastructure Works Program ("any physical capital assets in Canada instrumental in the provision of public services") was too vague:

> This wide definition [of infrastructure] has allowed large projects typical of the "boosterism" tradition of municipal politics to be approved … it is faith or boosterism rather than logic that underlines these claims to links between economic development and infrastructure. What seems apparent is that the infrastructure program has been captured by the traditional municipal elites and that the effect of the program is to give them money to pursue their dreams.[9]

Or it could have something to do with what Donald Savoie, a professor of public administration at the University of Moncton, calls "cargo cult mentality":

> I think of it as the Second World War when Americans flew in with cargo planes to an island, I think it's in the South Pacific. Natives of the island had never seen a plane before, and the

Americans came, built an airstrip and all kinds of cargo planes flew in and unloaded good stuff — jeeps and food. So this silver bird would fly in and bring all kinds of good stuff. And the locals thought that's how it was done: you go out, clear a stretch of land, put some lights around it and a silver bird's going to come in. And that's a cargo cult. And the case should be made that in parts of this country we've had a cargo cult mentality — we've put in lights, sewers, water, industrial parks, streets and thought, "Now let's sit back and see the cargo come in."

In the modern-day version of this phenomenon the cargo is full of new businesses, prosperity and jobs for the unemployed. Good things everybody wants.

That brings me to the question of lobbying. Of course private construction companies were highly interested in a country-wide infrastructure program — especially in the early 1990s when the high rates of unemployment in that industry were causing much hardship.

When we were hired we were not specifically asked to investigate the relationship between politicians and lobbyists in the implementation of the infrastructure program. But the research done for one of Stornoway's previous projects, *Days of Reckoning,* demonstrated that businesses in Canada approach governments with their hands out — despite their free enterprise rhetoric.

It is important to mention that to a great extent those who benefited from the infrastructure program were the construction companies that got the building contracts, as well as the municipal governments that got the two other levels of government to chip in to pay for projects that were essentially municipal responsibilities.

One does not need to have studied the implementation of the infrastructure program in detail to imagine engineering and construction companies lining up to bid on the thousands of publicly financed projects.[10] Bridges and roads had to be repaired, community centres had to be built, sidewalks had to be laid down, water and sewer systems had to be upgraded. Considering that the infrastructure program ended up financing some 18,000 projects around the country, it is not hard to understand that the prospect of a nation-wide program had many small entrepreneurs salivating. They certainly didn't stand in the way of the FCM when the municipal organization pushed for its infrastructure-renewal initiative. And frankly, who could blame them?

Right. Nobody. Nor can you blame the cities.

Take the Saddledome. Calgary was pleased to include that project on its list because the city didn't have to pay for any of it. You see, the Saddledome Foundation (which is private) paid the municipal third of the total $12 million. That made everyone happy. The foundation got the renovations it wanted in the arena — private luxury boxes — and paid only one-third of the total costs. The city supported the renovations because they were a nice way to enhance, at no cost, a piece of property that the municipality gets to lease to other people.

With all these people saying how great these soft infrastructure projects were, who was left to criticize them?

Variations on a theme

What we learned doing this research into the Canada Infrastructure Works Program is this: If you want to do well as a governmental spending program, you gotta be sexy. Er, I mean, *politically* sexy.

In the 1980s when the Federation of Canadian Municipalities first came up with a plan to repair and restore the country's core infrastructure, it concentrated on the basics: roads, sewers, bridges. Unfortunately, this stuff isn't sexy. For one thing, most of it is underground. For another, core infrastructure is, well, boring. I mean, who gets excited when municipal workers put a new sewer under their street?

So as we saw in Chapter 1, the FCM had to go back and revise its approach. Former FCM president Ron Hayter told us how the federation did it:

> The [new] program that we put together was a three-pronged approach. We would concentrate on the importance of repairing the crumbling infrastructure of Canada. That was absolutely essential. Second, we were in the midst of an economic downturn in Canada, so we wanted to emphasize the importance of doing this work to create jobs at a time when a lot of people were out of work. And third, we wanted to emphasize the fact that good infrastructure in your community is important from the standpoint of attracting industry and business to your

community. It was part of making Canada more competitive. So that was the three-pronged approach that we used. It was a lot sexier than the approach we used in 1986 where we were only concentrating on traditional, basic infrastructure. The FCM adopted this new approach for its next thrust at the federal and provincial governments.

And guess what? It worked.

We wanted to understand the stark discrepancy between what had been promised and what ended up being delivered. Government officials were able to justify pretty much any project simply by claiming that facility X would bring tourists and that arena Y would contribute to the quality of life or serve a municipality in various ways. In short, projects such as tennis courts and bowling alleys were "good" and "worthy" endeavours.

Perhaps they were. But were they infrastructure? Yes, by the very fuzzy definition of infrastructure set forth by the government: "Any physical capital assets in Canada instrumental in the provision of public services."

The vagueness of this definition meant that everything in the program was subject to interpretation, with the predictable result that everyone had his or her own idea of whether or not one particular project was worthy of infrastructure funding. Consider what David Anderson, federal Cabinet minister, told us when we asked him to justify some of the questionable projects in his province of British Columbia:

Well, value for dollar depends on what priorities you have. And we were saying that we wanted projects to come from the municipalities: these were their priorities. And then these projects had to fit in with the overall provincial priorities.

"But wait," you might say, "politicians do need a bit of flexibility. Otherwise, no government could ever *do* anything."

Right. Governments need a little bit of flexibility. Governing a country cannot be as straightforward as making sure Little Sarah gets to school on time. Only we are not talking about a little flexibility here. We are talking about criteria wide enough for a Mack truck.

Go back a few paragraphs and re-read the definition of infrastructure. Pay attention to the wording. "Any physical asset." Do you think a hospital is a physical asset? Yes. How about a doghouse, a chair or an old, chipped coffee mug? These are all physical assets, are they not? An asset is something *useful* to which a value (*any* value) can be assigned.

"Hang on," you say, "it also has to be 'instrumental in the provision of public services.'"

OK, go get your dictionary and look up "instrumental." Chances are you will find something like this: "*adj.* to indicate that something is used for a purpose." If Fido could talk, he would tell you his house is definitely used for a purpose.

There is only one other thing left: our physical assets have to be used to provide a *public service.* As in, say, removing snow? Finding a cure for cancer? Teaching good table manners? There is no way of telling since the government has no agreed-upon definition of what constitutes a public service.

You get the point. The vagueness in the most important definition of the infrastructure program made it possible for politicians and bureaucrats around the country to do virtually anything they wanted with the $8.3 billion of public money devoted to that one particular program.

Which in turn makes it almost impossible for anyone (auditors general, journalists, ordinary citizens) to measure the success or failure of the infrastructure program.

What kind of accountability is that?

We certainly were not happy with this finding. As mentioned earlier, if we are to have an accountable government, we need to start with clear intentions and clear programs with relatively fixed criteria — all of which allow citizens to evaluate the performance of the people they elect to take care of public business.

We are not against the Outremont Theatre, the Calgary Saddledome or the nice folks playing bocce or bowling in brand-new facilities across the country. What we don't like is the fact that a program aimed at repairing core infrastructure was used to finance projects *other than* repairing core infrastructure.

In other words, our beef is that the results of the infrastructure program turned out to be different than what had been promised and advertised. We just wanted to know why. Maybe politicians made the right decisions. Who knows? We wanted to know whether the people in charge of delivering the program made the right decisions when they chose to fund such projects as the Jarry Tennis Stadium in Montreal, the Stanley Theatre in Vancouver, or the 37 community centres in Manitoba. As things stood, we couldn't even tell how they made these decisions.

When the rules of a spending program are vague and imprecise, nobody can hold the government to account. By using an unclear definition in the Canada Infrastructure Works Program, the government gave itself lots of room to manoeuvre. As a result, politicians could decide arbitrarily to use public money to fund projects that were *not* aimed at repairing Canada's crumbling infrastructure.

If you were the head of government and wished to avoid being held to account by citizens, you would start by using fuzzy declarations of intent. Nobody could be quite certain what you were up to, so they could not ask you harsh questions about the way you manage the nation's business.

What you could also do, just to make sure nobody could ever track any of your decisions, would be to set up cost-sharing programs in partnership with provinces and municipalities, and the programs would be implemented by bureaucrats from two or three different levels of government.

That would make for an incomprehensible labyrinth. Oh, what fun that would be!

NOTES

1. I wish to emphasize that I am not criticizing the worthiness of any of these projects. What we were concerned about was that they had nothing whatsoever to do with infrastructure but still received money from the Infrastructure Works Program.
2. The theatre actually opened in the spring of 2001.
3. Legendre was appointed Quebec minister of tourism, recreation and sport by Premier Bernard Landry in March 2001.
4. According to the *Ottawa Citizen*, the Quebec City convention centre received approval before the CIWP was announced in 1993; this approval coincided with the retirement of former Quebec health minister Marc-Yvan Côté, a long-time provincial Liberal from Charlesbourg, just north of Quebec City. See Elaine Flaherty, "Liberals relaunch $6B infrastructure program," *Ottawa Citizen,*

January 15, 1994, p. A4 and Joan Bryden and Eric Beauchesne, "Officials admit playing politics with $27M grant," *Ottawa Citizen,* January 6, 1994, p. A3.

5. Details on the bocce courts in North York: The Pleasantview arena renovation/addition cost $2.4 million, to heat and air-conditioned the bocce courts. The federal-provincial share paid was $1.6 million, with the rest kicked in by the City of North York. The Glen Long Community Centre required $1.6 million to replace its pool and enclose its bocce courts. The federal and provincial governments paid $1.06 million and the City of North York paid $1.06 million. The I. W. Chapley Community Centre got $1.15 million for a pool and two bocce courts, with the federal and provincial governments paying $766,667. The remainder was paid for by the City of North York. The Grandravine Community Centre received $2.6 million to add on to the centre, additions that included new bocce courts. In Phase I of the program the City of North York paid for 25 projects costing a total of $29.794 million.

6. Halsey-Brandt was elected as a Liberal MLA in the spring 2001 election in B.C.

7. Comments quoted in Canadian Press, "Federal government won't cater to NHL owners," *Ottawa Citizen,* March 17, 1994, p. D3.

8. We'll discuss the original proposals in Chapter 3.

9. Caroline Andrew and Jeff Morrison, "Canada Infrastructure Works: Between 'Picks and Shovels' and the Information Highway," in Susan D. Phillips, ed., *How Ottawa Spends 1995–96: Mid-Life Crises* (Ottawa: Carleton University Press, 1995), pp. 107–135.

10. Some of these companies donate money to specific political parties.

3. KAFKA'S CASTLE THREE TIMES OVER

The beauty of cost-sharing programs

One of my favourite novelists is Franz Kafka. He wrote haunting stories about ordinary people getting stuck in totally mindless mazes of regulations and bureaucrats. One of his novels, *The Castle*, is about someone who received a job offer in a remote area and decided to take it. Only he could not find out what he was expected to do without seeing the high bureaucrat in charge of his hiring, who kept evading the hero using all sorts of bizarre rules. This chapter will describe our visit to Canada's "Castle."

As we discussed in earlier chapters, the infrastructure program was a tripartite initiative. Federal, provincial and municipal levels of government were involved in implementing the program. The tripartite structure proved to be our most frustrating brick wall. Dealing with bureaucracy is never fun, and we got bureaucracy three times over.

You know what it means to be dealing with a bureaucracy. It means asking questions for which there *never* seems to be any possible answer — only multiple choices on your touch-tone telephone.

If you manage — finally — to talk to an actual human being, you usually get an incomprehensible mishmash of jargon irrelevant to your case. The person at the other end of the phone line does not know the answer to your question. Sorry about that, please try again soon.

When we were doing our research on the infrastructure program, we had to make gazillions of phone calls. Finding out why the decision to build community centre A instead of repairing bridge B was made turned out to be way more complicated than it seemed at first.

Conventional wisdom has it that when everyone is responsible nobody is responsible. When we asked questions of municipal officials, they referred us to the provincial department. When we called up provincial officials, they told us final decisions were made in Ottawa. When we asked federal bureaucrats — you guessed it — they sent us back to the municipal and provincial governments. For some reason we never seemed to be talking to the right person.

As we saw in Chapter 2, accountability needs clear definitions of roles and responsibilities. The question of "who does what" is crucial to assessing whether public money has been spent properly and according to the rules. Cost-sharing programs can have a devastating effect on accountability if there is no way to hold any single level of government responsible for decisions, and if questions are easily avoided because they can be passed from one level to the next. Within cost-sharing programs accountability is frequently lost in red tape and layers of bureaucracy because the lines of authority between the three levels of government are blurred.

And that's not all. As we will see shortly, there is no tripartite auditing system in place to deal with Canada's new fondness for tripartite spending programs.

To eyes other than ours the beauty of cost-sharing programs is that they allow each level of government to make its own wishes come true — at only half or one-third of the cost. They also allow politicians to get some mileage spinning said programs as benefits to the community. Why, cost-sharing programs enhance co-operation between governments, they favour national unity, they allow politicians to put money where it creates more jobs. And overall, they save money!

Don't take my word for it. Jill Vaughan, Manitoba director of the Infrastructure Secretariat, said tri-governmental programs are the way of the future because they reduce the load on the taxpayer. Also, they improve co-operation among the various governmental levels while giving citizens a better appreciation of the type of government involvement at each level: "It gives us an idea of some of their accountability requirements" ("us" referring to ordinary citizens and "their" to various levels of government).

Ms. Vaughan was by no means the only one to praise the virtues of cost-sharing programs. Manitoba finance minister Eric Stefanson, for one, made the tripartite process sound very tidy:

> In the case of Manitoba, representatives from the provincial government, the federal government and local municipalities were part of the whole decision-making process for individual projects. We allocated one-third of the money to projects outside Winnipeg, and we had a consultative committee of representation from the municipalities to give us advice on what projects to support. We allocated one-third of the money to the City of Winnipeg and we had the city give us advice on projects. We had the remaining one-third in what we call the "strategic allocation" — all of those recommendations came to me and the federal minister responsible, who would then make the final decisions on behalf of our government.

In British Columbia Don Littleford, the engineer responsible for the Annacis secondary treatment plant, also told us how swell the co-operation was among the various levels of government. Once the application for infrastructure funding was in, he said, the funds started flowing through. I guess that's a pretty good thing when you're in charge of such a large project.

But for all the praise, tripartite governmental programs are probably the *best* way for all parties involved to avoid accountability, by endlessly passing the buck between the different layers of bureaucracy. As Tully Clifford, manager of Calgary Transportation Services, put it:

> Through the national infrastructure program there's nobody, in reality who's clearly identified as the person responsible for the program from a political or even administrative point of view. So there is nobody. You could point a finger, but it would be at

nobody. That's a huge problem. We're accountable only to the program itself. So what we have to say then is that the projects did meet the guidelines and the dollars were there.... But at this stage there is no accountability back to the public. I am, for example, under no requirement to come back and say, "Here at the end of it is what happened in Calgary." We are planning on doing that to make it a matter of public record, but there is no requirement — none.

Cost-sharing programs are the most efficient way to sell government discretionary or distributive spending programs politically. A discretionary program is one in which the criteria are flexible. The infrastructure program is a very good example, as we saw in Chapter 2. Old Age Security is an example of a non-discretionary program: if you reach a certain age and your income is below a fixed level, you are entitled to a monthly cheque of X dollars. With distributive programs decisions are made in such a way as to "distribute" benefits relatively evenly across the different regions of the country.

Cost-sharing programs are very popular with politicians because every level of government takes the benefits while no one takes responsibility for mistakes or dubious projects. In the case of the infrastructure program the federal government got the credit and publicity (something we will discuss in Chapter 4), the provinces got the money from the federal government and municipalities got big flashy projects built in their cities.

And no one was ever seriously reprimanded for goofy decisions and questionable projects. Provincial governments referred our questions to the federal level (who had initiated the program). Ottawa returned our questions to the provinces because they were the ones implementing the program. The municipalities met our questions with blank stares and rambling answers, telling us that municipal politicians were not sitting at the table when the decisions were made.

It was a nightmare.

And our difficulties were not the result of our inexperience as researchers; even seasoned politicians ran into the same problems. One official in P.E.I. plainly asked us to drop him a line if we were able to find out how decisions had been made (the decision-making process was a mystery to him). Surrey mayor Doug McCallum confessed he had no clue who he could phone to get an explanation as to why his city received money to build unwanted bike paths. And in Richmond, B.C., Mayor Halsey-Brandt admitted:

> I can't get any answer as to why [some projects were selected]. We just give [the CIWP decision-making committee] the information, and they disappear into a black hole and then you wait for the press release to come out to see who the winners and losers were.

It seems odd that mayors had to wait for press releases since the municipalities were supposed to be *partners* in this program. Not that this situation was specific to British Columbia, as Geoff, our researcher in Toronto, found out when he studied the National Trade Centre:

> We sit back and we look at this project and say everybody's co-operating, isn't that lovely? And to a certain extent that is nice, but it doesn't necessarily mean that something works because everybody is co-operating. The federal government had an eye on certain opportunities with regard to getting into the Trade Centre project, and Metro Toronto also had an eye on certain opportunities.

If mayors could not get answers to questions about *their own municipalities*, how could we, ordinary researchers with precisely zero political clout, expect to find anything?[1]

And how can *you,* the ordinary taxpayer, find out why authorities chose to build a new community centre instead of repairing that darn pothole-ridden Main Street?

The answer is, you can't. For two major reasons: one is the buck passing that goes on among the various levels of government; the other is "bureaucratese," the often complicated and incomprehensible language of government and its officials.

At some point during my research in Quebec I had a crazy idea. Was this language a version of Orwellian Newspeak? I had noticed the government officials used a vocabulary different from the one I was used to — new words carrying unclear meanings. So I said to myself, "Try to speak like them. Try to act as if you were a member of their club." I gave it a try and, lo and behold, things worked a little better. Somehow they recognized the words I was using. Maybe they thought, "Hey, it sounds like she knows about *this* ..."

Who said research wasn't fun?

But seriously, something had to be done. I was getting nowhere with my simple questions. I had spent an awful lot of time talking to officials, bureaucrats and politicians, trying to understand the way these people think. As I said, things worked a little better once I started walking and talking like them, but I soon realized that even they didn't always understand everything they were talking about. They reminded me of kids coming home from school and reciting their history lesson — "That day this thing happened, that day this thing happened ..." — but without making much progress in terms of connecting the dots.

Euphemisms, convoluted jargon and a great deal of hot air characterize this third official language of Canada. When speaking bureaucratese, politicians and officials talk and talk, but they never seem to be getting anywhere. The language of government makes the workings of government incomprehensible to the average Canadian.

The infrastructure maze

Take the rules of the infrastructure program — a complex maze of regulations, if ever there was one. For one thing, agreements between Ottawa and the provinces differed from one province to the next. As far as we could understand, control of the program was split between various provincial departments, depending on the province. Municipalities would send their proposals for projects up to a management committee with provincial and federal representatives on it. Some provinces allowed municipal representation on their management committees; other didn't. The management committee would then make a final decision on which projects to fund and which projects to dump.

At the federal level, control of the infrastructure program belonged to the Treasury Board. No one could explain to us why the Treasury Board, which is not a line department (it normally busies itself signing government cheques and overseeing employer-employee relationships within the civil service) was in charge of delivering the program.[2] The only reason we could see was that the Treasury Board president, Art Eggleton, was familiar with the infrastructure file —

he's a former mayor of Toronto and former president of the Federation of Canadian Municipalities.[3]

So federal control was left to the Treasury Board. But that was only *general* control. Regional control, as far as the federal government was concerned, was left to Ottawa's regional development agencies: the Atlantic Canada Opportunities Agency (ACOA), Western Economic Diversification (WED), the Federal Office for Regional Development — Quebec (FORD-Q) and so on. These federal regional agencies were named the *implementing agencies* for the program.

OK? You're still with me?

On top of that, there was an interesting twist in the arrangement. All the projects selected by each province's management committees had to be submitted to the minister for infrastructure (none other than Art Eggleton, the president of the Treasury Board). The interesting part of this additional rule was that the CIWP agreements that Ottawa signed with the provinces made no mention of the fact that projects had to be submitted to the Treasury Board.

Now, you might be thinking that because it was the management committees that made the funding decisions in each province, we would only have to check out the minutes of their proceedings to figure out why some projects were selected and others were not. Surely the committee members were recording was said during their decision-making meetings. I mean, school boards do, municipal councils do and neighbourhood associations do. *Everybody* who holds meetings keeps fairly detailed records of what went on during them.

I thought so too. But I was in for a surprise.

I would soon learn that our governments don't work quite the way school boards do. The minutes from the management committees were one of five things: 1) nonexistent; 2) too vague to mean anything; 3) secret because of federal rules; 4) secret because of provincial rules; or 5) secret because of municipal ignorance.

To make a long story short (especially since we'll talk more about secrecy in Chapter 5), the minutes from the management committees were utterly useless to us. So we were forced to go through the unspeakably long and tedious process of making countless phone calls to all sorts of government agencies and municipal councils to find out how decisions had been made under the infrastructure program.

Our quest for information about decision making proved complicated. Jay's first calls were within the Ottawa region. He started out by contacting City Hall to get a list of the projects funded under CIWP. Jay is a thoroughly adorable chap, but in this case he had to make a pest of himself. Why, he had to wait several weeks for some of his calls to be answered (others still haven't been).

"It's funny," Jay said to us at some point. "The only quick response I received was when a worker with the city thought I was calling to apply for infrastructure funding."

After this first unsuccessful attempt Jay decided to try something else. He spent much of the following winter hunched over maps, cross-referencing the municipalities with their federal ridings (a task not facilitated by the fact that the ridings had been changed after the 1993 election — eliminating a few, adding others and changing the boundaries on all but a handful).

"And then," Jay said, "after having sorted out more than 5,000 Ontario projects I came across several communities with the same names listed in the 'applicant' column, although there was no way of telling the towns apart. There were even place names in the government lists that I could not locate on any of my maps."

Frustrating? Yes. But there was more to come.

Jay's next move was to use a story from *The Globe and Mail* that claimed infrastructure spending favoured Liberal ridings over ridings held by other parties. He called the Treasury Board asking for information that broke down the projects by political party, only to be told that no such information existed.

That's when Jay started filing Access to Information requests. He asked for the material that had been released to the reporter who wrote the story. The Treasury Board sent him a list showing that a disproportionate amount of money had indeed gone to Liberal ridings. But the Treasury Board's documents also showed that *The Globe and Mail* reporter had failed to consider one significant detail: Quebec, which was heavily represented by the Bloc Québécois, and British Columbia, which was weighted toward what was then the Reform Party, were late handing out infrastructure money. This fact explained the inequity.

In that note Treasury Board officials claimed the sorting of more than 15,000 projects was a one-time endeavour that had not been updated. Jay later discovered that the Treasury Board had not broken down the projects by political party, but had in fact sorted the projects by riding.

"That's when I learned my first lesson in bureaucratese," said Jay. "When you request information, use the *exact* words. Do not say 'party,' say 'riding.'" Is this splitting hairs? Oh no — not when you're dealing with bureaucracy.

All researchers went through this "learning" process. In one of her weekly reports Anette, our researcher in Winnipeg, chronicled her collisions with the bureaucracy in her search for simple answers to simple questions:

This week gave a whole new meaning to spinning around in circles. I could easily describe the majority of efforts trying to cut through the red tape (not just scotch tape, but rather the thick, insulating stuff). Let's take one example, a classic one. Let's look at the attempts to locate any information on jobs created and dollars spent through the infrastructure program. First I contacted Winnipeg's Social Services Department asking for the infrastructure "Community to Work" file. "No, we don't have anything on that," I was told. "You should contact the Infrastructure Secretariat." I called the secretariat and was told that this office didn't have any files either, but I should call Norm Meier at the Public Works Department. Mr. Meier would be able to answer all my questions. So I called Norm Meier, who didn't seem to want to answer my questions after all. His colleague, Mr. Aubrey Hope (who initially didn't mind talking to me, but now, unfortunately, is stalling just like the rest), told me to contact the city's Social Services Department for any information on jobs and projects under "Community to Work." "Bingo," I told him. "I have spoken to people at the Social Services Department already and they don't keep any records either." This surprised Mr. Hope. And the name of my contact partner at Social Services, Mr. Juergen Hartmann, manager of employment and training, didn't ring a bell with Mr. Hope. So he guaranteed to look into matters and find someone I could talk to at Social Services. This was Tuesday. I gave him a couple of days to find a name and when I hadn't heard from him by Friday, I called him again. No answer; no hope. Similarly fruitless were my attempts trying to obtain tender lists for the Italian community centre. After requesting the list of tenders from the City of Winnipeg, I received a letter stating that because this isn't a City of Winnipeg project, I should contact the Italian Canadian Centre directly. I think the file drawers of the city must be awfully empty. No one seems to have anything on anything.

Anette was definitely spinning around in circles trying to find out who was responsible for doing what in the relatively small province of Manitoba. At one point she called Franklin Pitura, the minister of government services. His assistant told Anette that Mr. Pitura would not be able to give her information on the infrastructure program. "The minister of government services," she explained, "is responsible only for public buildings and not streets or community centres." The minister of finance, Eric Stefanson, was in charge of infrastructure funds and the minister of highways, Glen Findlay, was in charge of highways. Streets, Anette learned, were under the responsibility of municipalities.

Anette also tried to get specific numbers on the jobs created. She went to Social Services in Winnipeg to be told the information she was after was at the Infrastructure Secretariat. When she asked the people at the Infrastructure Secretariat, they in turn sent her back to Public Works. What did the people at Public Works have to say? That Anette had to go to … Social Services! Wheee!

While she was at the Infrastructure Secretariat, Anette asked whether the office could help her access minutes of meetings. The woman there said she could not. According to Anette:

I said, "How come we were able to access minutes in other provinces?" She was rather surprised about that. I asked, "How were committee decisions being made?" And she said, "Through regular meetings." I just wanted to get access to those meetings but they weren't available to me.

Sometimes we felt like we were right in the middle of a Dilbert cartoon.

As if this chronic lack of information was not enough, our contact people kept changing. So every time we talked to a new person, we had to explain who we were, where we were from, who we were working for and — last but not least — what we wanted. Mind you, it's not like we were getting an awful lot of help from our previous contacts, but having to deal with an ever-changing cast of bureaucrats did not make our lives easier.

For my part, the frustrating aspect of this job really was the way people at various levels of government kept asking me who I was, who I worked for, where I came from, etc.

In Calgary Lydia had a similar experience: "I have to tell them who I am, my entire background, who I'm working for and what I want to know. Why can't I, as a taxpaying Canadian citizen, just ask, 'How is it the decisions are made, what is the argument for funding one project over another, what are the benefits to the citizens?'" It happened to Jennifer too: "I did find that a lot of times people wanted to know a lot about Stornoway Productions, you know, tell me what it is, where it's coming from, what it's all about."

In British Columbia Leanne was having problems of her own with bureaucrats' attitudes. She got in touch with the Western Economic Diversification (WED) people, but they were not all that helpful. Bureaucrats would not agree to an interview unless they received the questions in advance. When Leanne got there to interview one person, three showed up. On top of that, there were a number of questions they refused to answer. As she put it:

> When I went to do the interview, they wouldn't even answer half my questions. Even stuff that's already in the public domain, such as this whole big scandal over transit in B.C. — the province basically tried to funnel a lot of the infrastructure money into transit and the municipalities weren't very happy about it. Everybody knows this scandal. WED knows that. It was in the newspapers. But when I asked them about it, all I got was, "I can't comment. Sorry, we can't talk about that."

Back to the minutes from the management committees. So far committee minutes had not been very useful to us; but we kept trying to access them in the hope that maybe we could find in them some clue as to how decisions were made under the infrastructure program.

In Montreal Philippe decided to take the bull by the horns. He was investigating the Outremont Theatre and he thought he'd start by going to the city library and reading the minutes from the council meetings on the subject:

> I went to the library and I read the minutes of the municipal council meetings. I did that for a whole week. I must have spent at least 30 hours reading the minutes of the meetings. And that gave me a pretty good idea that not much goes on in those municipal council meetings or that not much is recorded in them, that they neglect to write down a lot of stuff. There's a lot of expository dialogue but that's about it. There's not much information. They make references to stuff that isn't there ... even the municipal councils themselves suggested *in the minutes* that the minutes were poorly recorded. That's an interesting detail.

The same was true in Calgary, as the manager of Transportation Services, Tully Clifford, told us. He said minutes don't capture all of the discussion. Instead, minutes record the bottom-line decision. Much more goes on during meetings, one would assume. Unfortunately, the public doesn't get to see that by reading the minutes.

What is it that we ordinary citizens don't get to see by reading the minutes of governmental management committees?

Political games. Pressure tactics. Backroom strategy. The stuff that makes politics so — political.

If we could see what actually goes on in committee meetings, the first thing we would likely realize is that in order to receive funding for a project, one has to be *in the know*. We were wondering why a program aimed at repairing Canada's existing core infrastructure ended up funding such projects as the Stanley Theatre in Vancouver. We asked artistic director Bill Millerd how he had heard about the infrastructure program. He said the program was well publicized, and he knew the province of British Columbia was going to devote 15 percent of available money toward cultural projects. So Millerd and his people asked Tom Perry, their local MLA, to get an application form for them. Then they received "a great deal of help" from MP Hedy Fry to put in the application, although Millerd didn't specify what kind of help Ms. Fry offered.

Then, continued Millerd:

People on our board, like Ian Waddell, who was a former British Columbia MP, certainly knew the process and advised us not necessarily who to talk to, but who the minister responsible was. That person was given all the information. We did a lot of letter writing, and got assistance through the people in Hedy Fry's and Tom Perry's offices. They just assisted us in making sure that Premier Harcourt was informed. Premier Harcourt attended the Arts Club Theatre. We made sure [federal Cabinet minister] David Anderson was informed about the project and the quality of the project. We just got the word out. We were also very much helped by the press. The press said that it was a worthy project that should be supported. I think, from the politicians' point of view, they wanted those projects, it seems to me, that had a kind of high visibility. And the Stanley Theatre suited that, as did many other public projects … a politician would want to be seen as supporting that. I think, therefore, it's important, and also I got the impression that it was important in ridings where there was a Liberal federal politician and ... in the case of B.C., an NDP provincial politician. And fortunately Vancouver Centre, where the Stanley Theatre is situated, did have that at the time.

How important it is to know the right people. The same was true, by the way, in Toronto. North York councillor John Fillion explained to us how the business of horse-trading in Canada's world-class city was conducted:

It was the Capital Planning Committee that recommended to council what projects would be approved, and because nobody wanted a big fight on the council floor, the Capital Planning Committee was supposed to basically work something out so that it had eight votes to approve the package. So if you got frozen out by the Capital Planning Committee, you had eight votes against you, you weren't getting anything. That's what municipal politics is. There's always, within the group, a smaller group that's very good at controlling things and making deals and manoeuvring. And that group of politicians gets a disproportionate share of projects.

In case you haven't had enough, take a moment to read what Claude Ryan, the former Quebec minister of municipal affairs who was responsible for the infrastructure program until the fall of 1994 when the PQ returned to power, said to us:

> Take the Théâtre du Nouveau Monde. Mr. Gobeil, who was the president of the Treasury Board during our first mandate, was chairman of the board of directors and he had a great deal of interest in this project. He had convinced the minister of cultural affairs, Mrs. Lisa Frulla. Mrs. Frulla was very interested in a provincial cinémathèque project. As minister of cultural affairs, she wanted her portion of the cake. The theatre was the favourite project of Mr. Tremblay, who was the minister of industry and commerce. He was also the MNA from Outremont. So the city (Outremont), the minister, the MNA from Outremont and the minister of cultural affairs all favoured this project. Put yourself in the place of the minister of municipal affairs who was looking at this project. On what authority could I substitute my judgment for that of such real authorities and say, "I know what the needs of Outremont are, this is what it will be"? I was not made aware of other needs in the municipality of Outremont, whose fate I was not too worried about because it's a municipality that has the means to take care of its affairs and does not in principle need government aid.

All right, you get the drift. Politics is what it is because citizens allow politicians to play politics with their money. Citizens vote every so often for politicians who promise all sorts of nice things, and then these citizens go on living their lives, reassured by the thought of having responsible people in charge of public business. Only it doesn't quite work that way, and most citizens sort of know it.

Courting disaster

As we have documented in the case of the infrastructure program, accountability in tripartite government initiatives is often compromised. Furthermore, the resulting maze of informal, backroom arrangements is a recipe for disaster. You guessed it: tripartite government programs frequently lead to behind-the-scenes screaming arguments that end without satisfactory action.

Officially the infrastructure program was portrayed as a fine example of governmental co-operation. Officials from all over the country sounded as harmonious as a choir when trumpeting the successes of the program, what with all those bureaucracies "working together" and so on. Consider what Art Eggleton himself said in the House of Commons on January 21, 1994:

> Our success owed a good deal to the very co-operative attitude taken by all of the provincial governments. They have recognized the intrinsic merit of the program, they have responded to the public's desire for early action, and have shown a determination to demonstrate that federal and provincial governments can work quickly and co-operatively ... I also wish to underline the importance of the support this program has received from mayors and other elected representatives at the local level across Canada. They have been supportive, they have been enthusiastic and they are very much equal partners.[4]

Unfortunately for Mr. Eggleton, we heard much nastier words on the ground. Not everybody was singing the same merry tunes. Two particular examples, Vancouver-area mayors and one lonely mayor in northern Manitoba, were clearly not happy with the infrastructure program.

In Thompson, a small community in Manitoba, Mayor Bill Comaskey was very angry at the way the infrastructure program was administered. His city wanted to apply for four different projects, but instead decided on only one of them — repairs to a 330-home subdivision that had collapsing sewer and water lines. The city received the go-ahead for the project, but instead of paying one-third of the costs, the municipality ended up forking over $2.4 million, while the other two levels of government only paid $860,000 each. There was apparently not enough money to approve the project in full. According to Comaskey:

> We were at the point where we felt that if we did not accept the amount that was approved by the secretariat, then we would lose the project. They had us under the gun. We had no choice but to go ahead with the program and pay the lion's share of the

project costs and shut up ... it was almost as if it was intimidation by the other levels of government. "Take what you're getting. Be happy you have it and get on with your life." I don't see the fairness there at all.

Mayor Comaskey complained to our researcher Anette that his municipality had not had sufficient say in how the program was going to be administered. That claim was dismissed by Manitoba finance minister Eric Stefanson, who insisted that recommendations coming from the municipalities went to both himself and the federal minister responsible, who would then make the final decisions on which projects were going to be funded. Mr. Stefanson thought this arrangement was reasonable and "very inclusive in terms of having input from municipalities."

In British Columbia several mayors had a similar problem with the way the provincial government was handing out infrastructure money, particularly in Phase II of the program. Vancouver councillor George Puil told us that municipalities were not involved in deciding which projects were necessary: "Consequently, the projects that were done were the projects that the various MLAs, MPs or the provincial government wanted done, not what the city felt was necessary."

Unlike most provinces, British Columbia did not have any system in place to distribute money equally across the province. Most of the other provinces made sure that ridings received relatively similar amounts of infrastructure money. Without such a system British Columbia was vulnerable to charges of spending infrastructure funds in particular ridings to gain political advantage. Surrey mayor Doug McCallum explained:

The intent was good, but I think the way that CIWP proceeded as far as deciding what money to put out was flawed. The program went with provincial governments across Canada as a source to distribute the infrastructure money. When you go with provincial governments, you bring politics into it. When you start to bring politics into the distribution of infrastructure money, then the program starts falling apart. Projects are distributed for political reasons rather than for infrastructure reasons, and that's exactly what happened in British Columbia. The B.C. government had political reasons for where and how they wanted to spend the money. That's why a lot of the money that came to B.C. really wasn't disbursed to the proper infrastructure projects that were needed in the province.

In Richmond Mayor Greg Halsey-Brandt gave a good example of how a program such as Infrastructure Works can start flying apart. When we asked him what sort of project had been chosen for funding in his city, he replied, "The only thing we've gotten so far is some bicycle-lane improvements that we never asked for … We really don't mind. We get the bicycle lanes. But they weren't on our list and it's all we got."

Was the program hijacked in British Columbia by a provincial government eager to get federal money to help push its own agenda? Well, it's hard to be sure. Mr. Halsey-Brandt, for one, wanted to know:

> As mayor, I made a couple of calls provincially and federally, to get clarification of projects, decision timelines, how much money's available — that sort of thing. I could get answers to the harder questions like "How much money is left?" But I couldn't get answers as to why — why you chose this project over that project. I couldn't get answers on those.

As I said earlier, most politicians love cost-sharing programs because they allow each level of government to make its own wishes come true — at only half or one-third of the costs. They also "create" jobs while giving an opportunity for politicians to get some mileage spinning said programs as benefits to the community.

Cost-sharing programs, in case you're curious, are not included anywhere in the Canadian Constitution. They are a political invention and the problem with political inventions is that the inherent checks and balances within the system don't necessarily apply to them.

And guess what happens when government is left unchecked? That's right: it can spend public money on roads to nowhere and other questionable projects. As MP John Williams, chair of the Public Accounts Committee, put it:

> There's not enough accountability in government today because we haven't been able to design forces outside government that are beyond the scope of government, that cause it to act in certain directions. Because remember, government, in the final

analysis, holds all the power. It can legislate any force out of existence if it so desires. It can change the public policy of a program; it can widen the public policy; it can lower the standards.

What we found during our research was a majority of politicians (at all three levels of government) saying how much they like programs such as Infrastructure Works. But whenever we asked pointed questions (as in "Who exactly made the decision to build the Jarry Tennis Stadium in Montreal, and why?"), we were met with blank stares and replies along the lines of "That's what the municipality wanted" or "We didn't have the final say over this" or "Well, we all had to compromise and here's the result."

But when Lydia asked John Williams, "Who do I vote out of office if I don't like a certain project?" Mr. Williams and his federal committee could not help:

> We can't ... hold the provinces accountable for their [programs and management]. If they decide that they're just a flow-through mechanism by adding their one-third share, that is their responsibility. We, as the federal government, can't hold them to account. They have their own public accounts committees, which hopefully will be doing their job too. As for the municipalities, they don't have public accounts committees but they have the local taxpayers who can say, "Well, it's my road that's getting paved or it's my bridge that's being built."

Right. So nobody really has the authority to audit and hold decision makers to account in such a tripartite spending program. But then, we thought, somebody must have been looking closely at the money before it went out. We could not believe three levels of government would agree to spend several billion dollars without making sure the money was spent for the right reasons and according to the rules that generally apply to public spending.

So we asked David Anderson, who said:

> Well, the money, before it goes out, is looked at by three levels of government. First, we would accept no municipal proposal unless, obviously, the municipality had agreed to it ... so the proposal was looked at by the municipality. The proposal was

looked at in terms of the budget by the provincial government — what were its priorities, what did it think fit in with a wider scheme. We then looked at it a third time. So before the money was spent ... there would be three levels of government in favour of the particular project.

Glad to hear it. Yet there seemed to be something missing, such as a cross-level system of oversight that would focus on the money before it was spent, and another cross-level audit system to look at how well the three levels of government had *together* managed the program. As John Helliwell, professor of economics at the University of British Columbia, pointed out:

> Doing a systematic evaluation of projects is always much easier when there's a single decision maker. Once you start getting too many people sharing in the financing, it gets pretty complicated. So in a better world than the one we're in you could imagine this multiple decision making leading to a more formal set of rules so that everybody could go away happy and say, "We've done a good job for the taxpayers." I guess in a way I'm more attracted by that second line of thinking that says that with several people involved you'd think the governments would have been more systematic to make sure the right thing was being done.

It's not that we don't like one or another group of politicians. It's not that we're unhappy about new bike paths or modern tennis stadiums. Our beef is that cost-sharing programs, because they're outside the system of checks and balances laid out in the Constitution, make it almost impossible for citizens to figure out where their tax dollars are going, let alone why.

Perhaps you're thinking, "I didn't know the Canadian Constitution had a system of checks and balances ..."

Well, yes, it does. The Canadian version of checks and balances is not as obvious as the one in the United States, where power is clearly divided between the executive (the president), the legislature (the House of Representatives and the Senate) and the judiciary, but it is there nonetheless. In Canada bills have to go through three different readings, one of which takes place in the Senate; and the government has to defend its policies and decisions during Question Period in the House of Commons. Also, the Canadian Constitution specifically divides powers between the federal and provincial governments. The constitutional division of powers explicitly describes who is responsible for doing what in our system of government.

Canada is a federation. The main characteristic of all federations is that they have a mix of independence and interdependence. Federalism reconciles unity and diversity by allowing the central government to take care of so-called national matters while protecting local rights and the autonomy of the provinces. Properly functioning federalism is an important source of predictability in public law — citizens have a way to know which level of government is responsible for what.

In every federation legislative powers are divided between central and local governments (there may also be a few areas of concurrent jurisdiction). In Canada most legislative powers are assigned exclusively to either the federal or provincial governments, while such powers as immigration or agriculture are shared by the two orders of government.

The constitutional division of powers was a *sine qua non* for the provinces to accept Confederation back in the 1860s. They wanted a written guarantee that their local rights and autonomy would be protected and respected. The provinces (especially Quebec and Nova Scotia) were afraid of losing their powers and autonomy to a central government. The division of powers was the solution: a guarantee for the provinces that their autonomy in so-called "cultural" matters (education, language, religion) would be protected.

So historically the constitutional division of powers was needed to bring the four founding provinces together into Confederation in 1867. But for our purposes here, the division of powers is important as a mechanism of accountability since it tells citizens who is responsible for doing what. For example, if you are not happy with education policies, the provincial government is the place to seek changes.

It sounds clear in theory, yet we keep hearing that the federal government regularly invades or encroaches on provincial jurisdictions. How does it do that? Two major ways: residual powers and spending power.

Residual powers provisions in the Constitution allocate jurisdiction over those matters not otherwise listed. The Founding Fathers had to include a clause allowing one level of government to regulate "new" areas, such as telecommunications or aeronautics, for example.

In Canada residual powers are assigned to the federal government. Our Constitution also provides the federal government with specific override or emergency powers to invade or curtail, in certain conditions, what would otherwise be provincial constitutional powers. The federal government, according to section 91 of the Constitution, is entitled to "make laws for the peace, order and good government of Canada, in relation to all matters not coming within the classes of subjects by this act assigned exclusively to the legislatures of the provinces."

The inclusion of these four words — peace, order, good government — in the Constitution has resulted in 130 years (and counting) of jurisdictional battles between the provinces and the federal government. The notion that only Ottawa could deal efficiently with certain social matters, regardless of the powers conferred upon the provinces by the Constitution, was as prevalent in the 1870s as it is today.

Federal invasion of provincial jurisdiction is nothing new. It started in 1878 when the federal government tried to implement a national Temperance Act. The justification for the act was that it promoted public order and safety, but in fact it affected property and civil rights, an area of provincial jurisdiction.

The first person to challenge the national Temperance Act was Charles Russell, convicted of unlawfully selling liquor in Fredericton, N.B. The case made its way to the Judicial Committee of the Privy Council in Britain (the highest court for Canada at that time). The court ruled in 1882 that the federal Parliament could legislate for the peace, order and good government of Canada pretty much as it pleased, even if it meant encroaching on provincial powers.

Thus we see from the beginning a tendency of both Ottawa and the judiciary to give a broad interpretation to the legislative capacities of the federal government — even at the expense of provincial powers. The 1882 ruling introduced what is known as "the aspect doctrine," a fancy expression meaning that the federal Parliament is allowed to "affect" areas of provincial jurisdiction if the effects are simply "incidental" to the main purpose of a federal law.

The ruling of the Judicial Committee laid the foundation for more than a century of court rulings allowing the federal government to stretch its legislative powers at the expense of provincial jurisdiction.

Federal social laws involving employment insurance, health care, old age pensions and so on are prime examples.

Not to say that these programs are unnecessary or ill advised — on the contrary, most Canadians view the social safety net as one of the most valuable aspects of their life in Canada. But the fact that these laws are popular or necessary should not make us forget that they affect provincial powers, sometimes significantly. They also make it more difficult for citizens to hold their various governments to account because such programs are in fact blurring the lines of responsibility between the different levels of government.

The other major source of federal encroachment on provincial jurisdiction is what is known as the "spending power."

The spending power is exactly what its name suggests. Regardless of constitutional division of legislative powers, any level of government can spend money in any way it wants, as long as it has the consent of its legislature to do so.

Even though they have the power to spend money in areas of federal jurisdiction, the provinces have not shown any tendency to do so — for reasons having to do with limited resources and increasing needs in their own areas of responsibility. The federal government, on the other hand, has spent significant amounts of money in areas of provincial jurisdiction, especially in the case of social programs.

Most federations around the world allow their central governments to spend money in areas of subsidiary jurisdiction (provinces, states, cantons, etc.). The American, German, Swiss, Australian and Spanish constitutions all contain explicit provisions to that effect.

The Canadian version of the spending power we know today first appeared in the 1930s during the Great Depression. Provinces in those days did not have much money to face the skyrocketing needs of their populations. Social assistance to unemployed people became too heavy a burden for the provinces, so the federal government stepped in.

We know the rest: provinces slowly became dependent upon federal money in areas of provincial jurisdiction such as social assistance and health care.

As tempting as it may be to criticize the federal government for encroaching on areas of provincial jurisdiction, we have to keep in mind that there was probably no other option available to politicians at the time. Citizens were desperate for help their provincial governments could not afford. There was also the example set by the American government with its New Deal. And there was no institutional check within the federal government that could have prevented, or at any rate slowed down, its invasion of provincial jurisdictions.

This lack of checks on the use of the federal spending power in Canada has led to the institutionalization of transfer payments (which today represent roughly 20 percent of provincial revenues) and to the mushrooming of cost-sharing programs such as medicare, the Trans-Canada Highway, the Canada Assistance Plan and … the Canada Infrastructure Works Program. Yes, we've come full circle: a federal program aimed at repairing roads and sewers is clearly stepping into municipal and provincial jurisdictions.

"But then," you may wonder, "why is it that provincial and municipal politicians didn't raise a storm? Why is it that every politician in the country gladly went along with this program?"

The answer is that local politicians *wanted* the federal government to get involved in local infrastructure.

Politicians love cost-sharing programs for very good reasons: walk a mile in their shoes and you will understand why these programs are so popular among our various governments.

First, politicians at all levels of government can tell taxpayers that their level is only paying a portion of the costs. What's better for a local politician than funding only half, or better yet one-third, of a local project while getting his or her picture in the newspapers? That's right: politicians from all three levels get a share of the credit during photo-ops and ribbon-cutting ceremonies.

Another reason why many politicians love cost-sharing programs is that no single level of government is entirely responsible for any decision. As our researcher Leanne said, "No one has ever said in my entire research, 'Yes, I am responsible for this decision. I am responsible for this project.'" When something goes awry, it can usually be blamed on someone else. Lydia would certainly agree:

> I thought the job would be easier than it was. I thought that I could make a few phone calls and things would work out quite simply, you know, people would tell me the answers I wanted

to hear or at least give me an answer. It was a lot more frustrating than I thought. And it was also difficult to be treated with such suspicion. I'd never encountered people being so suspicious of my motives or who I was or what I was ... I had to justify my existence and defend myself, when in fact I was asking them questions.

Granted, we were not exactly ordinary citizens. Not everybody gets paid to devote two to three months (and in the case of Jay, years) trying to unravel government decision-making processes.

Still, no doubt the average citizen is confused. In such a program, where different levels of government "co-operate," it becomes virtually impossible for anyone to find *the* level of government responsible for *one* project. Municipalities say final decisions are made at the provincial and federal levels. Provinces say municipalities propose projects. Federal officials say that it is the provinces that ultimately decide what kind of projects are selected and how they act vis-à-vis their municipalities.

When faced with this kind of treatment, most citizens will simply shrug and forget about accountability altogether, as we were all tempted to do during our research. If cost-sharing programs are aimed at discouraging citizens from asking questions of their politicians, they certainly do a good job.

Our Constitution divides legislative powers between the two levels of government. The main reason for this division is the protection of provincial rights and autonomy within Canada. But a constitutional division of powers is also an important mechanism of accountability — it tells citizens exactly who is responsible for what. If politicians neglect to respect established jurisdictions, citizens end up with a complicated, multilevel scheme of governmental decision-making processes. Sort of like Kafka's Castle.

In a way cost-sharing programs put the federal nature of Canada in jeopardy. They make the constitutional division of legislative powers — the cornerstone of federalism — seem irrelevant. Citizens want goodies and services; governments team up to deliver them. In the process, lines of responsibility are blurred and accountability is lost in layers of red tape and bureaucracy. We lose our ability to question and hold our politicians accountable, mostly because we lose track of who is responsible for doing what.

Losing track … hey, that's what happened to us!

NOTES

1. Our research opened our eyes to a very interesting paradox. While municipalities were very influential in policy making (as we saw in the previous chapters when we discussed the Federation of Canadian Municipalities), they seemed to be rather helpless in the actual implementation of the CIWP program.
2. A line department is a department with which citizens interact (Human Resources, Justice, Veterans Affairs) or one whose regulations affect most of us (Environment, Citizenship).
3. This raises at least the possibility of an institutional — as opposed to a personal — conflict of interest.
4. Canada, Parliament, House of Commons, *Debates*, January 21, 1994.

PART TWO

The Road Less Travelled Leads to Funny Places — En Route to Ottawa

4. BY THE PEOPLE FOR THE MOMENT

What does a member of Parliament do?

After having spent months investigating the infrastructure program, we were still not quite sure who had made the decisions to fund particular projects rather than others. We could often find answers to what, how much, where and so on. But we could not find out why.

We knew the program was a federal initiative — it was an important element of the 1993 Liberal *Red Book*. So we went to Ottawa to seek answers to our questions. We went to where power is concentrated to try to understand how it is exercised.

We wanted to talk to members of Parliament because they are the ones elected to represent the citizens. MPs are the direct link between citizens and their government. They're also vested with the most important aspect of government: control of the public purse.

Yes, that's right. In theory MPs are the ones who control how public money is spent in Canada. If any institution can bring about accountability, it is the House of Commons. Our constitutional theory is crystal clear: the government cannot spend one cent without the approval of the House. If money is wasted or ill spent, then MPs should face the consequences since they are the ones who approved the spending.

John Williams, chairman of the Public Accounts Committee,[1] explained to us:

> In the concept of Parliament the parties do not exist; we talk about parliamentarians, those who support the government and those who oppose the government. But the concept of Parliament is not broken down into clear party divisions, that these MPs support the government and these MPs are in the opposition. It talks about parliamentarians supporting the government's initiatives, and if the government can carry the day in the House of Commons, then it has the confidence to govern. But this has evolved into this tight party discipline that says if you are a member of the government, you will vote their way regardless of whether you like it or not, and that allows them to stay in power even though perhaps they maybe really do not enjoy the confidence of Parliament. But by the vote it appears that they do.

We were not naive enough to believe MPs were entirely responsible for the way public money was spent under the infrastructure program. We knew about the politics of party discipline and the realities of Cabinet government. We were not expecting to find independent-minded MPs voting according to their consciences or the wishes of their electors without paying attention to the party line.

We asked some MPs how they managed to balance their theoretical duty to supervise government spending with the very practical issue of party discipline. Why would they be interested in looking at budget documents? What kind of incentive is there for back-bench or opposition MPs to do so when party discipline determines how government and opposition MPs vote?

MP Jason Kenney didn't mince words:

> If you think the MPs are a cornerstone of democracy regarding the public purse, you're awfully naive. Ordinary MPs might theoretically be the bastions of democracy, but in practice the

best we can do is ask questions, usually not get answers, raise concerns that usually aren't listened to.

For her part, Bloc Québécois MP Suzanne Tremblay didn't seem to have a big problem with party discipline within her own caucus. Why not? Because, she says, she is part of it. She is working together with other Bloc MPs to build a party line, and all MPs in that party seem to participate in the final decision as to where they stand. Everybody has to make concessions, she said. Only there are exceptions: "If there is a party line that I cannot support at all, I won't be in the House to vote against it; I will stay in my office rather. But I will never stand up to vote for something or against something if I don't personally agree with it. I won't be in the House at that time."

Asked whether being absent for the vote wasn't simply another way of voting for the party line, Mrs. Tremblay replied that this sort of thing is very rare:

> To be in politics there is a line, a party line, and if you don't go along with the party line, you may be excluded. We take your portfolio, we say you're no longer the spokesperson for that, you're punished. And I think it's not worthwhile because I think it can be useful for Canadians, being a spokesperson for Canadians. So I think it's better to stay in my office rather than to say, well, I'll stand up and vote against my party. Look what happened to Mr. Nunziata and others that were members of the Liberal Party who decided to vote against the government. The political parties don't support this kind of rebellion in people.[2]

As I said, we didn't go to Ottawa with hopes of finding MPs in full control of government spending. But we were surprised to realize how little power or influence an MP actually has. So little that most of them have simply given up trying to influence public spending, especially when it comes to cutting expenses. Instead of fighting the prime minister and his Cabinet, most MPs find themselves scrambling from one photo-op to the next, emphasizing the number of jobs created by the government and the importance of the government playing a significant role in achieving this, that and the other thing.

Politicians love to cut ribbons. Everybody knows that. And the fact that they often fail to look beyond the next election is not exactly a big surprise. What did strike us as worrisome was the realization that MPs play no significant role whatsoever in ensuring that questions are asked before money is spent, that sufficient and effective monitoring occurs during program delivery and that results are evaluated after the money is gone.

Not that this is anything new to those who follow public affairs. Over the last couple of years newspaper readers have witnessed an increasing number of commentaries and criticisms about the slow erosion of the power of the House of Commons. MPs are "chopped liver," said former Canadian Alliance House Leader Chuck Strahl. They are nobodies in the House of Commons, according to former Liberal-then-independent MP John Nunziata. "It emasculates democracy when you marginalize individual members that have been democratically elected," said Conservative House Leader Peter MacKay in October 2000.[3]

What does this situation mean for citizens? What exactly should the representatives of the people be doing in Ottawa? If the members of Parliament cannot bring accountability into government, who can?

That's a question our researcher Leanne put to Bloc Québécois MP Stéphan Tremblay. "How are we going to give power back to the MPs and to the people?" she asked. "I think the population in general will have to care more than they actually do," was the young MP's reply.

So citizens have to care more about how public affairs are managed in Ottawa. But they can only do that if they can access relevant information about what their government is up to. Citizens also need to understand a few key principles of our British-inspired system of parliamentary government.

But where do I, as an average citizen, start to understand how government works? Alliance MP Rahim Jaffer offered this response when asked how citizens could understand government by tracking where their tax dollars go:

That's the bigger challenge. Most people lose interest after about the first few steps when they have to trace where that dollar goes because it has to go through so many different levels of bureaucracy before it actually gets to the end. And I don't know what the ratio is today, but I know that at one point the dollar, every dollar collected from the taxpayer, literally only less than a third of that would actually end up going to something. ... So in the end I think I would encourage all Canadians to try to understand government, try to see especially the inefficiencies of government. I think a lot of people just generally throw up their hands and say, "Oh, you know, it's not even worth looking at it."

How long do we have to keep running around in circles?

One of the most crucial aspects of our system of government is the "business of supply." This expression refers to the rules governing the raising and spending of public money. These rules, although relatively easy to understand, are very special and crucially important because they relate to the conduct and maintenance of government itself. In short, the business of supply is at the heart of government.

In the early days of Confederation Parliament's role as guardian of the public purse led to the creation of two institutions designed to help parliamentarians fulfill their duties: the auditor general and the Public Accounts Committee. They exist to make sure the government reports dutifully on its use of public funds and to review whether public money was spent for the approved purposes with due efficiency, economy and effectiveness. Question Period in the House allows opposition MPs to call the government to account for its use of public funds. Though it is not part of the institutions of government, the media, by reporting on mishaps and scandals, is another mechanism of accountability: it puts pressure on the government to report on its use of public money and forces disclosure of information by government officials.

Let's have a closer look at the institutions that help our elected representatives fulfill their duties as guardians of the public purse.

The Office of the Auditor General

The Office of the Auditor General dates back to 1878, when former Liberal member of Parliament John Lorn McDougall of Renfrew, Ontario, was appointed the first independent auditor general of Canada.[4] At the time the job of the auditor general (AG) was twofold: 1) to examine and report on past transactions, and 2) to approve or reject the issue of government cheques.[5]

You might think it strange that the person responsible for reporting on government spending was also the one deciding whether or not a cheque would be issued. Sort of like investigating one's own past actions, it would seem. I guess Richard Bedford Bennett's Conservatives thought so too, because when they were in power in 1931, things began to change.

Under the Conservatives, responsibility for issuing cheques was transferred to a newly created government official, the comptroller of the treasury, while the auditor remained in charge of reporting on past transactions. This change drew a clear line between the duties of the government and those of the auditor, decreasing the potential for conflicts of interest: the government was responsible for collecting and spending public funds, while the auditor was in charge of examining and reporting on how those funds were spent.

The 1977 Auditor General Act[6] updated the role of the auditor general.[7] He or she would not only look at the accuracy of financial statements, but would also examine how well the government managed its affairs. In addition, the new act reasserted the old principle that the AG does not comment on policy choices but only on how policies are implemented.

This distinction is very important. The Office of the Auditor General is an instrument for achieving accountability, not for criticizing policy choices or the politics of governing.[8]

The way the auditor general helps achieve accountability is by closing the loop in the business of supply mentioned earlier. Control of public money is carried out by members of Parliament, which means that the government must obtain the permission of MPs before raising taxes or spending public funds. After it spends public money on programs and services, the government must report on its use of the money to Parliament.

Given the complexity of government operations, members of Parliament need help from an impartial third party to decipher the information contained in the public accounts of Canada and the different financial statements tabled by the government, and to make sure that the information accurately reflects the results achieved by government programs and services. That's where the auditor general comes in. It is his or her role to audit government operations and hand over his or her findings to Parliament.

Because the auditor general is independent of the government of the day, he or she is in a position to help MPs fulfill their role as guardians of the public purse. The auditor general is appointed for a term of 10 years and has the freedom to recruit staff and set the terms and conditions of employment. Auditors general also have the right to ask the government for any information they require to do their job, and they report directly to the House of Commons, not to the government.

Public Accounts Committee

However, the auditor general is not the last word on accountability. You may have heard criticisms regarding the "two-day wonder" — the AG presents his or her report to the House of Commons, the newspapers cover the story on their front pages for a couple of days and then everybody forgets about it and nothing else happens.

To ensure that MPs examine the important points in the auditor general's reports on an ongoing basis, Parliament has created a House of Commons Standing Committee on Public Accounts. The work of the committee is based on the AG's reports: it reviews whether public money was spent for the approved purposes with due regard to efficiency, economy and effectiveness. If the committee finds that government spending did not meet these criteria, it makes suggestions as to what should be done to rectify the situation.

The Public Accounts Committee was established during the first Parliament of Canada in 1867. Since 1957 an Opposition MP has chaired the committee. As John Williams explained:

> Public Accounts is the committee that holds a government to account. Unlike the other committees that deal with policy and are looking to resolve problems and developing solutions for our society, Public Accounts focuses strictly on government on a retrospective basis of what went wrong. Why did it go wrong? What are we going to do to fix it to ensure that the taxpayer doesn't end up being taken to the cleaners for mismanagement, lack of accountability and waste of the taxpayers' dollar? So Public Accounts focuses on all areas of government. We start off with an opening statement by the auditor general outlining his synopsis of his chapter, followed by a presentation by the appropriate

committee, the deputy minister, giving his rebuttal and explanation as to why things have gone off the rails, and from there it's opened up to questions where all members of the committee, government members, opposition members, all parties, have the opportunity to ask the questions that they think are important. And from there that record is transcribed. We have two researchers working for us and they take the testimony that we have received, including the questions raised by the members, and they prepare a report, brought back to the committee for us to debate and we debate it in camera, so we come to hopefully an agreed-upon report. We then table that report in the House of Commons, and from there the government is required to respond within 150 days as to the recommendations that the committee has tabled with the government {about} resolving the problems that the committee sees. So there's a full circle. The auditor general does a full investigation, lays the facts before our committee. We call in the auditor general and the department; we hear both sides at the same time. We then prepare a report, table it in the House of Commons; the government must respond. If the committee doesn't like the response, we can call them all back again and start the process again so that there is accountability.

OK, so that's how things are supposed to be working once the money has been spent. Now let's have a look at the institutions that look at the money *before* it goes out. Apart from individual MPs, who are supposed to be the ones watching the public purse by questioning the government and voting on government budgets, pre-spending institutions include the Treasury Board Secretariat and the Office of the Comptroller General.

The Office of the Comptroller General

As the name suggests, the job of a comptroller general is to control government spending before it takes place, for example, by making sure expenses incurred by departments don't exceed or depart from the purpose of their budgets as voted by Parliament.

As I mentioned earlier, the Office of the Comptroller General of the Treasury was established in 1931 by the Bennett government. According to Donald Savoie of the University of Moncton, the purpose of this office was "to set up an elaborate system of 'commitment control,' designed to ensure that funds were spent only for the purposes for which they had been voted and that departments would not overspend their budgets." As Mr. Savoie wrote in his 1990 book *The Politics of Public Spending*:

> The Office of the Comptroller had, at its peak, close to 5,000 officers scattered in all departments, all regions and abroad. These officers were responsible for examining all expenditures prior to payment. They were instructed to withhold approval and refer to Treasury Board any expenses which in their view were not lawful charges against appropriations and to report when any department had overcommitted a vote.
>
> To carry out these responsibilities the office kept elaborate records of all outstanding commitments and expenditures. At the beginning of each fiscal year the office established a breakdown of each vote approved by Parliament. These breakdowns were known as allotments and usually corresponded to the standard objects of expenditures as set forth in the details of the estimates that departments presented to Treasury Board for approval. Accounts were then set up in the books and the amount approved entered in each account. When expenditures were submitted for certification, the amount was deducted from the account. In this manner the comptroller always had a running balance for each vote and each account and knew the uncommitted balance, the portion committed but unspent, and total expenditures to date. Departments had a duplicate accounting system in place to monitor their spending.
>
> Whenever proposed expenditures exceeded the amount in the account, only the Treasury Board could authorize new funding or, as much more frequently happened, a transfer of funds from one account to another could be effected by increasing one account and decreasing another.[9]

So the job of the comptroller general was to control spending before it took place, and the auditor general (and Public Accounts Committee) would review and report on spending after it had occurred.

Unfortunately, the effective powers of the comptroller general have been significantly reduced as a result of administrative and procedural changes in the late 1960s.[10] The comptroller general is now part of the Treasury Board Secretariat.

Treasury Board Secretariat

This institution exists to help the federal government "manage its human, financial, information and technology resources prudently and in a manner that best supports the government's objectives and priorities." As the administrative arm of the Treasury Board, the secretariat has a dual mandate: to support the Treasury Board as a committee of ministers and to fulfill the statutory responsibilities of a central government agency. The secretariat is headed by a secretary-comptroller general, who reports to the president of the Treasury Board.[11]

Those concerned about how the government looks at public money before it is spent should consider the "Comptrollership Branch" section on the Treasury Board's Web site. It explains how this branch helps government officials deliver affordable, quality services to Canadians using various accounting and risk-management methods. The only problem with the comptrollership branch is that its job description is rather vague. Its goal is to support "getting government right," but unlike the description outlined in Mr. Savoie's book, there is no clear sense of exactly how it is supposed to control public money *before* it goes out.

So now we've come full circle — we're back to the business of supply.

The business of supply

Think of the $175 billion taken every year from the pockets of ordinary Canadians. Think about your paycheque: how much of that money do you actually get to keep? Roughly half perhaps. We're talking approximately 50¢ out of every dollar. Where does the rest, the other 50¢, go? Government coffers at all three levels. It would be nice to have some say as to how this money — your money — will be spent, right? Well, that's exactly what the business of supply is about.

In British constitutional theory, upon which our Canadian Constitution is founded, the House of Commons plays the role of the "grand inquest" of the nation. The House judges government's proposals for national expenditures and grants supply accordingly. In other words, the Canadian Constitution gives control of the public purse to the members of Parliament.

Citizens elect MPs to the House and give them control over how the government collects and spends their money. Citizens have the right and the responsibility to make sure MPs are doing a good job. Citizen monitoring of elected representatives — either directly or indirectly through various institutions — is one of the pillars of democracy; citizens have to know their representatives are performing their duties properly and doing what they said they would do with citizens' money. That is what accountability boils down to.

Parliamentary control over public money is twofold: the business of supply authorizes government expenditures for various programs and services, and the "business of ways and means" allows the government to raise revenues, usually by the imposition of taxes, to pay for these expenditures.

Holding the government to acceptable levels of accountability ranks among the principal roles that Parliament is expected to perform in our democratic system. The business of supply is a major vehicle through which Parliament ought to fulfill this role.

Nice theory, isn't it?

Well, we thought, if MPs are the ones who control how government raises and spends public money, then MPs are the ones who will be able to answer our questions about the odd projects financed through the infrastructure program. So off we went to Ottawa.

But our trip turned out differently than we had expected. We were not so naive as to believe MPs held all the power in government; but we thought we'd get to meet at least a few of them who could tell us something — someone who could give us a more satisfying answer than "It's not up to me."

We were more than disappointed. Very few of the MPs we spoke to thought they were responsible for the way government raises and spends public money. Why is there such a difference between theory and practice?

In fact, the discrepancies between the theory and practice of parliamentary control of public money have many causes. One is that the size of government relative to the economy has exploded — from 15 percent in

1926 to 46 percent in 1996. As the size of government increased, so did the extent of its intervention in the economy, making it more difficult for MPs to keep track of public money. In addition, ministers introduced more and more demands for money in the House; this increase in the number of demands presented a serious challenge for MPs trying to review and control government expenditures.

The time limits imposed on the opposition's right and duty to question government proposals for expenditures also contribute to the discrepancy. Government rules for studying estimates started to change in 1913, with the introduction of closure.[12] Closure allowed government to gain supremacy in time, scope and organization of debate. The opposition could no longer talk bills to death; filibusters were practically outlawed.[13] New rules in 1927 further stated that no member other than the prime minister, the leader of the Opposition, a minister moving a motion or the first member to reply to a motion was to be allowed to speak for more than 40 minutes.[14] Apart from time limits on debates, the rules governing the study of estimates by the House remained essentially unchanged until the 1960s. Members of Parliament would debate the details of the government's spending propositions on a line-by-line basis in the House of Commons. Ministers would routinely be required to stand up and defend their spending decisions before Parliament. This procedure gave ordinary MPs a chance to participate fully in the budget process and act as watchdogs of the public purse.

During the late 1950s and early 1960s the explosion of government expenditures (in response to increasing demands from citizens for social programs and services) made it impossible to study the budgets and estimates on a line-by-line basis. Also, it was not in the spirit of the times for ministers and top-level bureaucrats to spend most of their time arguing over financial and accounting details. The business of supply required 90 full days (three months!) in 1965–1966. Many in the government thought it cumbersome to devote so much time every session to the supply process. Much more interesting was the prospect of building a modern nation.

The fairly strict rules of budget planning in Ottawa at the time caused tension and led the government to set up the Glassco Commission to make recommendations on updating management and oversight structures in government.

The report of that commission, released in 1962, called for more flexibility in government and the devotion of less time to the long and tedious process of budget review. Instead of debating each line of the budget in the House, the report said, it would make more sense to move these discussions into specialized committees.

It took a few years for the government to implement the changes recommended in the Glassco Report. In 1965 Lester Pearson's Liberal minority government obtained opposition agreement to a rule change that shifted budget estimates debates from the floor of the House of Commons into parliamentary committees. The changes also set a limit of 36 days for supply. These 36 days were eventually cut down to 20, ending by June 23 of every year. Only eight votes per day could be held during the 20 days allotted to the study of estimates. Crucially, any other budgetary items or motions on the agenda for that day not actually voted on would be "deemed" to have been passed by the end of that day.

The 1968 changes made it impossible for members of Parliament to delay the granting of supply. Timetables were introduced that prevented the opposition from slowing down the government. By June 23 of each year, whether or not Parliament had voted on the motion, the government would receive its funds because the budget would have been "deemed" passed.

Sure, the introduction of a financial calendar made the business of governing Canada more efficient. But it also removed the most important safeguard against the arbitrary use of state power by the people in government: the possibility for the House to reject expenditures.

For instance, one very interesting yet disturbing discovery we made during our research was how casually the funding for the infrastructure program had been granted. We're talking about a sum of more than $2.5 billion initially (at the federal level alone). That money came not from an act of Parliament, but was simply rolled into the general budget of February 1994. What this means is that the infrastructure program was lost in a sea of other expenditures and MPs did not get the chance to scrutinize it properly.

Another cause of the discrepancy between theory and practice when it comes to federal spending is the mind-bending complexity of government expenditures. Even Government House Leader Herb Gray complained in 1994 that estimates were complex and difficult to analyze, that the rigorous timetable made the examination of estimates rather cursory and that there was no focus for parliamentary debate on government spending before its priorities were actually set.[15]

Paul Dick, Ottawa Valley MP from 1972 to 1993, explained just how complicated a job it is to study government estimates:

> Estimates today are in a form which 99.9 percent of the population in this country haven't a clue how to read. It's a third language. It's not French. It's not English. It's accounting but nobody understands it! I got the managing partners of each of the six major accounting firms in the Ottawa area to sit on a committee with me and help me try to develop this theme. Five out of the six said that they did not understand the government's accounting or the government's books, and that they could not read them. The other one admitted that he did understand it, but he had worked in government for 10 years.

True, most of us find any kind of financial statement tedious, complicated or both. That's why we hire accountants. But when you take the pointlessness of studying government estimates that are for all practical purposes already set in stone and you add in the inherent complexity of financial statements, you end up with MPs who very rationally opt out of the whole process. They find something else to do with their time instead of worrying about complicated things over which they can have little influence, if any. Ordinary MPs have nothing to gain, politically or otherwise, by trying to act as watchdogs for the public purse.

Because MPs can no longer refuse money to the government, the government is more "efficient" — it cannot be paralyzed or defeated by a negative vote on some aspect of the budget. But accountability has been sacrificed for this efficiency: MPs no longer exercise their constitutional role of guardians of the public purse, and citizens have lost their most important safeguard against potential mismanagement of their tax dollars.

But then we wondered: if MPs are no longer worrying about the budget, what are they doing?

"One of the first things I noticed when I started this project," Jay told us, "was the emphasis placed on selling the infrastructure program to the public. There was nothing subtle about the governments' efforts. The desire to sell this program to the public was not confined to any one region of the country nor was it peculiar to any level of government or political party in charge. It was very widespread."

And, indeed, most of the infrastructure program documents we looked at were related to the public relations aspect of the program.

Remember how useless the minutes from the management committees were to us? These minutes were not, however, completely free of information. They were enlightening in at least one way: although we couldn't find any record of committee debates that decided which projects would receive funding, we did find out what the public relations campaign in such-and-such municipality was meant to look like.

It almost seemed, in fact, that members of the committees spent more time organizing photo opportunities for politicians than they did debating the validity of the specific projects before them.[16] We even came across a huge media analysis study detailing what the media in every city in the country had to say about the infrastructure program.

So do our findings suggest that our MPs do mostly PR stuff? We looked around when we were doing our research and I have to tell you that there were an awful lot of plywood signs across the nation — huge billboard signs singing the virtues of this or that politician or project. Why? Is this what we elected our MPs to do?

We asked Tom McMillan, a former federal Cabinet minister. "Politicians love to cut ribbons," he said. "They love to have big, four-by-eight-foot plywood signs extolling the virtues associated with them by virtue of roads, sewers, bridges and all such things."

Right. But what we *really* wanted to know was this: Why did so many MPs seem to be singularly focused on these roadside signs — as opposed to watching the national purse?

Mr. McMillan continued:

You see, the federal government by definition is heavily involved in areas where it's very difficult for federal politicians to get credit. There's not much political credit at the ballot box for foreign aid, for national defence, for research and development, for bilingualism or whatever program you might want to mention in association with the federal government. But — excuse the pun — roads, bridges, sewers, wastewater treatment plants, things of that sort, are concrete. They're up front. People can see them. They drive on them. They go by them. They can certainly see a great big four-by-eight-foot red-and-white sign saying this is our gift to you, courtesy of the federal government and the local member of Parliament in particular. If he's a Cabinet minister or she's a Cabinet minister to boot, all the better.

Mind you, we found the same kind of enthusiasm for big plywood signs at the other two levels of government. Ruth Grier, a former Ontario Cabinet minister in the NDP government of Bob Rae, told us quite candidly how she would never turn down an opportunity to be on camera. Only, she said, photo-ops don't necessarily work as well as intended:

> The public wants to see the library built; it wants to see the park improved. It will thank anybody who happens to be around at the time it happens, but not for many people is it a vote-determining issue.

Grier's comments seem a bit odd. Most politicians love the "visibility" aspect of their job. Yet they suspect (or maybe even know) that visibility is not necessarily vote-determining. I'm not sure I understand. Politicians are in the business of winning elections. They do everything they can to get elected, and then they set about doing everything they can to get re-elected. But the main tactic they're using does not quite work.

It's beyond me.

Let's go back to the case of Thompson, Manitoba. As you'll recall from Chapter 3, Mayor Bill Comaskey was very angry at the way the infrastructure program was administered in his community. His city finally settled on a project involving sewer and water lines in a 330-home subdivision. The municipality of Thompson had to fork over $2.4 million while the two other levels of government only chipped in $860,000 each. Strange, considering that the infrastructure program was supposed to be a tripartite agreement in which the three levels of government split expenses equally. So we thought we'd ask around to see how the federal and provincial governments had treated other municipalities in Manitoba.

Our researcher Anette met Winnipeg mayor Susan Thompson during a ribbon-cutting ceremony for the opening of the Pavillon Gallery

Museum — a $2.25-million renovation project financed under the infrastructure program, with one-third of the cost paid for by a prominent citizen. Anette noticed that the on-site sign failed to mention the participation of the City of Winnipeg, even though the mayor played a prominent role in the opening ceremony. She asked Mayor Thompson why her city didn't get credit for its contribution to the project. The mayor explained that the city provided two subsidies to the project but none under the infrastructure program.

As Mayor Comaskey told us:

> I believe that the program was heavily influenced by politics. The governments [federal and provincial] wanted to take an enormous amount of credit for the program, leaving out the municipal level of government. The municipal level of government is the first order of government. It's the government closest to the people. We were really looking for credit for the program. We wanted to get the job done. We were offended by being left out of the parade.

While the project was under way, the municipality of Thompson received a very colourful sign from the other levels of government, to be installed at the location. The sign prominently recognized the Government of Manitoba, the provincial minister responsible and the Honourable Lloyd Axworthy, federal minister responsible for the project, but made no mention of municipal involvement. Understandably, Mayor Comaskey felt that Thompson had been left out — and it was doubly frustrating for him since his city had to pay the labour cost of having the sign installed.

Not to worry, said the other levels of government. You will be supplied with a nice brass plaque to commemorate the project. As Mayor Comaskey recalled:

> As we were getting close to the completion of the project, discussion continued on the actual bronze plaque, the size of it and the wording of it. I was told that the wording would include Canada-Manitoba Infrastructure Works Program, the date and the ministers responsible, the Honourable Lloyd Axworthy and the Honourable Eric Stefanson. But no mention of the City of

Thompson. I said, "Just a minute, this is a partnership. It's actually a tripartite agreement, and the plaque will not go up unless it includes the City of Thompson."

The squabbles were far from over. The official ribbon-cutting ceremony had to be rescheduled several times. And on the big day they could have had the official opening in a phone booth. Elijah Harper, then the local MP, did not attend. Lloyd Axworthy was absent too. As for provincial representation, Eric Stefanson turned down the invitation and decided instead to have then-MLA David Newman represent the government. There was a twinkle in the mayor's eye when he told Anette that the permanent brass plaque still sits somewhere in the basement at City Hall.

Likewise, things were not all that rosy elsewhere in Manitoba. We spoke with Jae Eadie, deputy mayor of the City of Winnipeg and a past president of the Federation of Canadian Municipalities. He said that at the very beginning of the program in Manitoba, municipal governments weren't recognized on the signage. For instance, the first few signs that went up on tripartite projects in Winnipeg didn't recognize the city's contribution. In order to get municipal bureaucrats in touch with the provincial and federal bureaucrats, Mr. Eadie "raised a little hell with our own administration." While this situation may remind you of the tri-level mess we discussed in Chapter 3, it appears to have worked out quite nicely in the case of Winnipeg. Immediately after Mr. Eadie raised his "little hell," the signage was changed. "We had to change the culture of the other two orders of government right at the very beginning because, somewhat typically, they wanted our money, but they didn't recognize that it was contributed by us," concluded Mr. Eadie.

Signs, signs, signs. We encountered so many of them during our research that we started to feel a tad obsessed with the issue. Was credit taking the *sole* concern of our politicians? In Ontario Ruth Grier said something that didn't help us shake off our increasing sense of discomfort. It seemed that communications and public relations (photo opportunities, signs, etc.) were more important to various levels of government than making sure the city, province or country was being governed properly:

> Certainly the signs went up on the projects. We set up a committee to administer the program that had two federal rep-

resentatives, two provincial representatives and a representative from the Association of Municipalities of Ontario. So projects were vetted by that committee and that was really where the responsibility lay. Then there was a communications unit which was only federal and provincial people working on the announcements. I think it's entirely legitimate that both levels of government wanted to get the credit for what was going on.

Jennifer, our researcher in Eastern Canada, found an interesting gentleman we came to refer to as "The Sign Man": Jack MacAndrew. He explained that his company had something called a "standing offer" with the federal government. (A standing offer is simply a system in which the government hires a company or individual to find businesses to contract out government work.) In this case MacAndrew had to find a company to erect infrastructure signs.

In the winter of 1997 Mr. MacAndrew was contacted by the Atlantic Canada Opportunities Agency (the agency responsible for implementing the infrastructure program on behalf of the federal government in Atlantic Canada). The ACOA wanted Mr. MacAndrew to find a company to put up around 50 signs across Prince Edward Island on specific infrastructure projects. "Clearly," he said, "the federal government was very interested in taking as much credit as it could."

But was this only a matter of taking credit? Couldn't we say those signs were intended to inform taxpayers about the various projects being built under a public program paid for by their own taxes? Mr. MacAndrew didn't think so:

> I cannot imagine any other reason to put up a sign saying, "We are responsible for this benefit to your community," other than to achieve direct benefit at the voting booth. That clearly had to be the aim. I participated in that process because they called me to do it and I had the standing offer. Somebody had to do it, so I did it. But the thought of spending money on these dumb signs which litter the countryside … You know, if you can't do better than that as a government to make people think you're doing a good job, I really don't think that the signs are going to even achieve the ultimate effect.

Once again it seemed we were running around in circles. Visibility is not necessarily a good way to win elections, yet politicians kept engaging in visibility "contests," conducting themselves as though plywood signs and ribbon-cutting ceremonies were the only things that mattered to Canadians. As UBC professor John Helliwell put it, the successful MP is the one who can show well-paved roads.

Or maybe the visibility game is part of a larger plan devised by the federal government. As Tom McMillan explained:

> They've been extremely skillful at marketing the infrastructure program as a benefit to the taxpayer, even if it doesn't make an awful lot of sense in terms of public policy. Politically speaking, it's a gift that keeps on giving. In fact, if you go into any constituency in this country, chances are you will see a big plywood sign, sometimes red and white, sometimes other colours, advertising that this, whatever this is, is the gift of the federal government. In many cases that sign has been up since the 1993 election, even though the relevant project may long since have been finished. It's excellent politics. It is superb marketing. It is wonderful electioneering because it's geared to the next election. But it is certainly not good public policy. That isn't to say that infrastructure by definition is not good. Obviously it is. It's required, but the way in which it's done, it's probably the last way that you want to devise it if you were doing it exclusively or even primarily from a sound, logical, sensible public policy point of view.

Political marketing vs. public policy. Electioneering vs. repairs to Canada's core infrastructure. Short-term gains vs. long-term planning. Politics vs. good governance.

Who makes those decisions, and why?

We consulted Michael Brooks, an infrastructure expert in Toronto. We wanted to have his view on how the infrastructure program fared in terms of public policy and good management. He summarized the program using only one expression: "political short-termism":

> What you would look at is a political party in power that makes decisions that are going to be implemented and reacted to within its term of government. So you have situations where a

politician might not want to make a decision that's going to carry over to the next term because his or her party might not be in power, and then the next party will get credit for it. Everybody wants to make a decision that's going to come to fruition within its term.

Could political short-termism explain why various governments decided to build such questionable projects as the ones we discussed in Chapter 2 (Stanley Theatre, Calgary Saddledome, Jarry Tennis Stadium)? And if politicians make decisions to fund certain projects and not others simply because they bring them more visibility, then what happens to Canada's already crumbling infrastructure?

McGill professor Saeed Mirza gave us an answer to that question that is not reassuring. He said that many politicians see only what is visible. They repair potholes or they have roads surfaced so that people in the riding are happy. But they ignore the areas of infrastructure that are hidden from their view in a "what you can't see won't hurt you" sort of way.

What politicians don't see is the many water systems in Canada that routinely lose clean water through leaking pipes, or the sewage systems that overflow during heavy rainfalls, leaking contaminants into the local environment. Some municipalities still lack the technology or ability to ensure that their drinking water is safe for human consumption. If a tragedy like the Walkerton E. coli outbreak is not high enough a price to pay for political visibility, then nothing ever will be.

Most Canadians seem willing to tolerate a certain amount of political games and pork barrelling. However, when we allow politicians to use public money primarily to boost their popularity at the polls, we pay the cost of political short-termism.

MPs are the constitutional guardians of the public purse; they should be the ones to keep a close eye on how the government spends our tax dollars.

Before government can spend one cent, it needs to have the consent of the House of Commons. The government first has to seek legislative authority for any spending program. Once a program has received this authority, the government must present estimates to the House for MPs to vote on the corresponding appropriation acts. Once these acts have been passed, the government can proceed with its spending.

That's the theory.

In practice things are rather different. The auditor general routinely finds cases in which MPs have been lax in their responsibility to review how the government spends taxpayers' money. Successive governments have amended parliamentary procedures in order to make the granting of supply more "efficient." Government controls the House through party discipline, ensuring a clean vote in favour of government expenditures. Government must report to Parliament on its use of money, but government officials control almost all of the relevant information.

On top of that, citizens do not seem to put much pressure on their MPs to control public spending. In general, voters do not reward accountability and responsible management. Instead, they evaluate their elected representatives by the goodies they bring back to their ridings.

As outlined above, government has to seek legislative authority for spending programs. In the case of the infrastructure program, legislative authority was established by an order-in-council on December 22, 1993, which allowed the president of Treasury Board and minister responsible for infrastructure to enter into contribution agreements with the provinces and territories. One order-in-council was issued for each of these agreements. Orders-in-council emanate directly from the government without having to go through a vote in the House of Commons.

And yes, this *is* a problem since the role of the government is to govern and implement programs *after* receiving the approval of a majority of MPs. The role of the Public Accounts Committee and the auditor general is to make sure the government did what it said it would do with public money.

Our Constitution gives the House of Commons control over public money before it is collected and spent. The auditor general and Public Accounts Committee examine whether the government has spent money according to conditions agreed upon by Parliament. But when the conditions of a spending program are imprecise (as was the case with the infrastructure program, as we saw in Chapter 2), then meaningful evaluation by the auditor general is almost impossible. As a result, there is very little accountability in the system.

As John Williams explained:

> Our system has become [unaccountable] because it's so adversarial and because discipline is so tight; the slightest mistake is blown up into the greatest of proportions. Therefore, the government will expend all efforts, regardless of the cost and benefits, to try and minimize and bring mistakes down to the barest minimum or none at all. That's why they're not interested in public policy being too well defined — because programs don't always achieve what they're designed to achieve. So if you don't set out and say, "This is what I really want to do," if you don't articulate that, then obviously the program is a success because they spent the money. That's the thing. Governments don't want to be held accountable because we set the benchmark so high that the slightest mistake is a huge embarrassment.

When we decided to go to Ottawa to find answers to our questions, we were not really expecting to find MPs sweating over the details of budgetary estimates and other such things. But we did expect that they would know a thing or two about their constitutional role as watchdogs of the public purse.

To be fair, some did. Tory MP Scott Brison, for one, reminded us, "There was a time when estimates were debated in the House of Commons, you know, line by line. Ministers had to defend spending on a line-by-line basis in the House of Commons."

When Jennifer asked Liberal MP Gerry Byrne about going back to a line-by-line study of estimates, he replied:

> You know what? It would be a perfect strategy because it would lull everybody to sleep, including you. If you want everybody in Canada to sit in front of their television screens while Scott Brison and Gerry Byrne debate line by line a $150-billion-a-year budget, we can do it, but I guarantee you, you're giving the government free rein and a free cheque.

We were not hoping for much — and that is exactly what we got. Instead of MPs fulfilling their constitutional duty as the "grand inquest" of the nation, we found politicians hungry for visibility and short-term gains.

And we still didn't have answers to our questions.

NOTES

1. We will see what this committee does further along in this chapter.
2. In April 1996 Liberal MP John Nunziata voted against the budget because it failed to abolish the GST. He was booted from caucus.
3. Quoted in Tom Arnold, "Chrétien criticized for marginalizing back-benchers," *National Post,* October 10, 2000, p. A9; See also Justine Hunter, "The quiet seat at the back of the house," *National Post,* October 9, 2000, p. A6.
4. Before 1878 a government official, the deputy minister of finance, performed the auditor general's job.
5. The reports of the Auditor General back in the late 19th century listed every government transaction "from the purchase of boot laces to contracts for bridge building." See www.oag-bvg.gc.ca under "What We Do."
6. The Auditor General Act is available at www.oag-bvg.gc.ca/domi-no/reports.nsf/html/97aae.html.
7. Further amendments to the Auditor General Act in December 1995 established the position of commissioner of the environment and sustainable development within the Office of the Auditor General. These amendments also imposed an obligation on government departments to publish annual sustainable development strategies.
8. Next time you read the AG's report, remember this: he or she cannot criticize political choices. Political discussions are off-limits. Politics is for politicians. Accountability and reporting are for auditors.
9. Donald J. Savoie, *The Politics of Public Spending* (Toronto: University of Toronto Press, 1990) pp. 50–51.
10. The power of the Office of the Comptroller General was decreased as a result of the Royal Commission on Government Organization (the Glassco Commission), which also prompted changes to the rules governing the study of government estimates by the House of Commons.

11. See the Treasury Board Web site: www.tbs-sct.gc.ca/wwa/tbs-mand_miss_e.html.
12. "Closure" refers to the usually unilateral government decision to end parliamentary debate on a question.
13. To "filibuster" is to obstruct a legislative assembly, usually by prolonged speaking.
14. Thomas A. Hockin, "Adversary Politics and Some Functions of the Canadian House of Commons," in Schultz, Kruhlak, Terry, eds, *The Canadian Political Process,* 3rd Ed. (Toronto: Holt, Rinehart & Winston of Canada, 1979) pp. 329–330.
15. Canada, Parliament, House of Commons, *Debates* (February 7, 1994) p. 962.
16. Keep in mind: three levels of government means three different sets of politicians to co-ordinate.

5. A CULTURE OF SECRECY

Are we looking for nuclear secrets?

During our research, as you may have noticed, we encountered many brick walls. Not only were we never talking to the right person, there never seemed to be a "right" person to talk to — someone who could offer any help or explanation about the decision-making process under the infrastructure program.

We started out by investigating a whole bunch of seemingly uncomplicated projects in six different provinces. We were constantly told, "Go there, call this person, come back here, sorry I can't help you, try calling City Hall, etc." And boy, did we ever spin in circles. I don't know the exact number of people in total we talked to but it was a lot.

Unable to find answers at the local level, we gathered in Ottawa, hoping our MPs would be able to shed some light on how the infrastructure money had been spent, and why.

We filed several requests under the Access to Information Act. When we received the documentation, most of the pages had been heavily censored. No explanations were offered. Nothing seemed to work, but it was not for lack of trying. As Anette said:

All of us travelled through Canada; we did extensive research and asked some very simple questions referring to the infrastructure program. We simply wanted to find out why certain projects were financed under national infrastructure and others were not. Who made those decisions and based on what criteria? Guess what? We all got the same answers. So this means there's no transparency for me as a citizen at the grassroots level. On to the next level: we find on provincial government levels no one knows and is not giving us any answers either because they don't know or don't care. Next level is senior government level, here, right now, Ottawa representatives. We find the same answers. Where is accountability?

And after going through all this trouble we still didn't know where the accountability was. Which is why we started doubting ourselves. We questioned our skills as researchers. We wondered whether we had asked the right questions, whether we had looked hard enough for someone who could explain to us the workings of the various governments in Canada.

But were our questions really so complicated? I mean, we were just ordinary citizens trying to understand the inner workings of a governmental program aimed at repairing Canada's roads and sewers.[1] We were not asking for nuclear secrets. We were not even criticizing government decisions.[2] We only wanted to know how the program had been implemented. Why such a cloak of secrecy? Were we a threat to national security? We certainly felt that we were treated like one.

Access to information?

While writing this book I came across an interesting article by Philip Preville in *Saturday Night* magazine.[3] According to him, 19,294 Access to Information requests were made in 2000 at the federal level alone. Roughly a quarter of those were filed either by reporters or by people working in politics. The remaining 14,000 or so were split between businesses and the general public.

The way Access to Information law works is this: when you want to find something that might be in the government's big file cabinet, you simply fill out a form and pay a $5 fee. Five dollars is a starting price;

you may have to fork over much more depending on the amount of research needed to dig up the documents you want.

The government is supposed to get back to you within 30 days — delivering the information or telling you the requested information is unavailable or classified.

Of course, we're talking bureaucracy here, so you can expect delays. On top of delays, the documents received are frequently incomplete or whited out — which means that you'll likely have to file more requests to try to uncover the information you need. If you're not happy with what you receive, you may file a complaint with the information commissioner. Out of the 19,294 requests filed in 2000, only 1,359 such complaints were registered, and only three ended up before a judge.[4]

The article in *Saturday Night* gave a real-life example of how these things work:

> In the last three years one researcher for the Reform Party/Canadian Alliance submitted over 1,500 Access to Information requests. (The party employs seven such researchers.) His requests generated over 200,000 pieces of paper and resulted, he says, in only 200 useful nuggets of ammo. That's 1,000 pieces of paper for each political bullet.

The Access to Information law proved pretty much useless to us. We were not in the same league as political researchers, but we did file quite a few requests. Jay alone filed over 75 of them. The responses often took months and months. In one case he waited more than a year for the government to release some of the documents related to his request.

Is *this* the best way for the government to show its citizens that it is committed to accountability and transparency? Or is it straight out of the BBC television series *Yes Minister*? — the episode in which Sir Humphrey explains to the minister that "You could have a good government, you could have open government, but you can't have both."

By and large, you can assume the government is not wild about delivering some of its information to ordinary folks. Delays are common, and most files you are likely to receive will have been "censored" by the authorities, with precious little explanation. The fact that the government might be reluctant to share some of its secrets is understandable in areas like national security. But information about the way in which choices were made to fund infastructure projects? Why are these things kept secret? Professor Helliwell gave us one explanation:

> Transparency's a good thing, but if the first person coming in with a question has got a camera and a headline behind them, then you can be very nervous about answering the question. To achieve transparency it's not simply a question of having disclosure of information rules that mean all questions have to be answered under pain of law. What you really mean is a system that produces enough information for the decisions, which usually end up in dry library files or on an Internet site or something, plus reports after the fact that allow anyone who's interested to see what the consequences were.

OK, so asking questions with a camera in tow is not the best way to get answers from politicians and bureaucrats. In politics, as I'm sure you know, embarrassment can be fatal. MP John Williams, for one, told us his Public Accounts Committee had derailed careers in the civil service. "Testimony in front of the committee," he said, "obviously demonstrated that some people were incompetent." In fact, the fear of being seen as incompetent or simply embarrassed by the release of "sensitive" information acts as a serious impediment to transparency and openness in government. As MP Jason Kenney put it:

> All the incentives are there to not release information. If you're a bureaucrat and you end up with a request for information on your table, it could be politically sensitive, it could embarrass the government or your department. Chances are you're going to err on the side of secrecy and not openness. And so over the years bureaucrats have, not maliciously but just out of self-preservation, built up a system of loopholes through which they keep information secret, keep it from public purview, because … they get no benefit from being open, but they do get the potential disadvantage, i.e., losing their jobs or not getting the promotion if they release information that's sensitive.

As a result, he said, "It's really impossible for somebody who isn't making the decisions to know how the decisions are made."

Accountability and transparency in government are obviously very important topics to us. We think that restoring accountability in government requires two things: 1) citizens have to inform themselves and keep asking for answers, and 2) the government has to be open to scrutiny. The fact that we could not find out how the infrastructure program's funding decisions were made was not an encouraging sign.

Perhaps we had been wrong all along. Perhaps the best way to understand the workings of the infrastructure program was not to ask politicians why they had chosen to fund some projects and not others. Perhaps, we thought, we should start with what the government said publicly and see where that might lead us.

"There was one objective," Jay said to us, "that was first among equals when it came to the Canada Infrastructure Works Program, and that was creation of jobs." Job creation, as you may recall, was one of the most important Liberal promises in the 1993 federal election.

The pressure to create jobs also came from various provincial governments. As former Ontario NDP Cabinet minister Ruth Grier told us:

> There had certainly been pressure on the federal government from our premier, Mr. Rae, as well as the premiers of the Maritimes to do something to create jobs. We found ourselves in the worst recession since the Depression and Ontario and the Maritimes were particularly badly hit. At federal-provincial meetings Ontario had been one of those urging the federal government to do something about jobs, and so the infrastructure program was announced.

Talking to both critics and supporters of the infrastructure program, we had the impression that the creation of jobs was not so much a beneficial side effect of repairing our infrastructure as a major reason for doing so. And yes, that makes a difference. If the idea is simply to create jobs, why bother with a huge national infrastructure program? Why not use the money to give subsidies to firms that create jobs instead?

For McGill's Saeed Mirza, it was clear that the infrastructure program was specifically designed to create jobs:

> If the federal government, along of course with the provincial governments, were genuinely concerned about the state of infrastructure in Canada, they would not have conceived such a program over such a short period. [Like] other issues in our society, health, education and social security, infrastructure is an issue that continues with us. It doesn't just stop after a period of five or six years. Infrastructure has to be maintained continuously. Infrastructure has to be rehabilitated whenever there is a need. Therefore, the governments have a responsibility to generate a policy stating that the quality of infrastructure enjoyed by Canadians shall be at [a particular] level.

We examined the job-creation aspect of the infrastructure program thoroughly. We looked at the claims made by all levels of government, but particularly the federal government. We also looked at the types of jobs government said the program created, and how the program may have affected private sector job creation.

Job creation was a very, *very* important aspect of the infrastructure program for our politicians. Maybe more important than repairing Canada's crumbling infrastructure. That was, at any rate, the impression we developed as we asked questions about oddball projects such as the Calgary Saddledome or Toronto's National Trade Centre. Whenever we asked how bowling alleys, convention centres, arenas, golf courses and community centres could be justified as infrastructure, we received responses that skirted the issue by emphasizing the impact on job creation.

All the researchers, yours truly included, investigated these job claims. Some of us ventured onto job sites to talk to supervisors and workers; some of us made calls to those in charge of administering the program.

Jay even took some time while on vacation in the Maritimes to stop by the Ministry of Municipal Affairs in Marysville, New Brunswick. "I wanted to put a human face on my Access to Information requests," he said, "hoping to speed them through the system." This was during the holiday season and, as Jay recalled, there was practically no one at the office:

> I drove there and found the parking lot almost empty when I pulled in and walked into the beautifully converted mill on the Nashwaak River. With a skeleton staff working the holiday week I was just happy to find out that there was someone to greet me and pass the word on that an Ontario requester had visited the office. This lonely public servant showed me a number of infrastructure applications, including one for an $80,000 subsidy to construct a FedEx building at the Moncton airport. A little voice inside my head asked me why a very successful American courier company was getting this subsidy to erect a building at the Moncton airport. When I peered down at the application I noticed that the line that was supposed to indicate the number of jobs estimated was blank. Considering no one had bothered to fill in the job estimates, I wondered how important the creation of jobs was when deciding which project merited funding. I stood there questioning how projects were decided and the public servant leaned over, as if talking to a co-conspirator, and whispered, "It's all political."

Ultimately, the federal government was responsible for the claim that the program had created over 120,000 jobs (most of them short term) across the country. As part of our investigation we decided to check out the government's arithmetic. We knew that the municipalities supplied job numbers to the provincial and federal governments when applying for a project. So we thought it would be fairly easy to get a rough count on the number of jobs created.

Lydia phoned the Treasury Board's communications advisor, Brian Biggar. She asked him what effect the infrastructure program had had on the overall jobless rate. His answer? "We have not done the calculations to show the precise number impact on job statistics. We can't do that; the jobless are fluid. It's a fluid situation."

He said he couldn't attach specific people hired through the infrastructure program to the job numbers because some jobs may have been part time, etc. He said 11,000 jobs were created in Alberta at the cost of $676 million. When Lydia tried to divide the number of jobs by the number of dollars, Mr. Biggar said, "You can't divide those numbers. Do you realize how much a bridge costs in materials to build?"

Granted, we're not experts in bridge construction. Besides, at this point we weren't investigating whether this program was an efficient way to create jobs. We were just trying to figure out how many jobs were created. The fact that we were having a hard time untangling this spaghetti is not a comment on our ignorance but on the difficulty of getting meaningful numbers from our various governments. As Lydia recalled:

> When I went to one of the job sites and I asked the supervisor, the superintendent I guess he's called, how many people he had hired, he said, "We hired eight to 13 people for the job." And I asked, "Were they new people or where did you get them from?" He said, "Oh, we got them at the union hall." When I think of union jobs, I think of high-paying jobs. And so really what we're doing is just inflating the union rates. We're making sure that the unions get paid and the only way you can get a union job is if you're a union card-carrying member. So really what we're doing here is just maintaining employment of the unionized sector. Which may be a valid argument, which may be something that we want to do. But this isn't how it was sold to the Canadian people during the 1993 election campaign. They said we were going to help the unemployed. And I would bet that none of those people were unemployed that actually got the job.

Had Lydia put her finger on it? Is this what the infrastructure program ended up doing: channelling funds to unionized jobs across the country? We could not clearly demonstrate it one way or the other.

Opportunity costs

All we wanted to do was to check the federal government's claim that the infrastructure program had created 120,000 jobs — did this claim equal the total of the various numbers provided by other levels of government? But why, you may wonder, would we want to fret over government numbers?

The first reason is that accountability starts with knowing whether the government did what it says it did. The second is opportunity costs: whether the money spent accomplished something worthwhile.

Think about it this way: you're having dinner with your family and you find yourself in the middle of a discussion about next summer's vacation. Instead of going to Europe this year, your father announces, the family is going on a road trip around New England. Why? Because this year your older brother Paul is going to college. You have only so much money to spend, so you have to make intelligent choices about how best to spend it. If your family blows everything on a summer vacation to the south of France, there won't be anything left for Paul's tuition fees.

It works the same way, by and large, with government. We citizens don't have infinite amounts of money to pay in taxes, so our various governments have to ask themselves good questions before they start blowing all we've got on questionable programs. And since government's money is everybody's money, each and every citizen has the right to question how that money has been or will be spent.

To check whether government's claims match reality we need information. If the government refuses to give us that information, then we start wondering whether it has something to hide. Why else would it be so reluctant to give us clear numbers on job creation?

While we were in Ottawa we asked Alberta MP John Williams for his opinion. Were we right in expecting transparency in government? Were we right in asking bureaucrats and officials to give us straight numbers on the job-creation aspect of a program as simple as CIWP? He thought so:

> Transparency is one of the fundamental ways of holding governments to account. We must have access to the process of their decision making and the facts that they have to arrive at their decisions. And when we find that decisions are made on a whim, on the back of a cigarette package or on no written basis whatsoever, just at the whim of someone, then we have to suspect, what kind of motivation was there to approve that?

Then Mr. Williams said something about undue influence in a non-transparent process that really stuck with me: "I'm not saying there was [such influence in government decision making] but you can't prove that there wasn't." That's right. Keeping information secret means that citizens cannot know for certain that there is no undue influence in the government's decision-making process.

So had the government done anything to figure out for itself whether or not the infrastructure program was an endeavour on which it was worth spending several billions of dollars in public money? Yes, as a matter of fact, it did.

After the first phase of the infrastructure program was completed, the federal government commissioned a study to find out whether it would be a good idea to implement a sequel. They hired a team of experts under the direction of University of Toronto engineering professor Richard Soberman. The report came out in 1996 and recommended that the government *not* go ahead with Infrastructure II. As though nothing had happened, the government then proceeded to go ahead anyway with the second installment of the program, raising the total cost from $6 billion to $8.3 billion.[5]

Among its many illuminating findings, the Soberman Report calculated the program's cost per job at $60,000. While the report stated that the jobs created were positive in that they were created for people who were "largely unemployed," it concluded that the result was only "modest improvements in the economy."[6]

Positive but modest. Good but not excellent. Gee, could they be more vague?

The more we searched, the more complicated things got. Reading the Soberman Report, we encountered a new term: "incrementality." Incrementality refers to a situation in which governments spend money on projects or programs that would not otherwise have been undertaken. Say you have an infrastructure program under which municipalities receive money to build new projects. If those municipalities use the new money to pay for projects that were already in their budgets, then there's no impact on job creation. In order to create jobs, you need to fund projects that were *not* already budgeted.

As it turns out, the infrastructure program was supposed to be incremental — but very few people actually cared to check whether municipalities were really using the money for new projects or merely financing projects that were already budgeted.

During hearings held after the first part of the program was over, Sue Barnes, a Liberal MP from London West posed some hard questions to Paul Thibault, the executive director of the infrastructure program and secretary of the Treasury Board. She wanted to know more about the levels of incrementality and the possibility that some governments might have inflated the number of jobs "created" under the program. She wanted to know, given the myriad possible variables involved in the jobs calculations, how the government could "be so definitive" with its numbers and claim with certainty that the program had created over 120,000 jobs across the country. Mr. Thibault's answer was rather puzzling:

> I'm not an economist, but I think you've clearly demonstrated that it's not an exact science. These are estimates. It's on the basis of what projects did not happen, but it's also on the basis of what would not have happened if the program hadn't taken place. Would there have been further projects discarded? One doesn't know. This incrementality business is not a very exact science.[7]

If incrementality is not an exact science, then trumpeting the number of jobs created under any kind of program is not an exact science either. The lesson here is that citizens should be skeptical of what the governments tell them and not take every claim for an absolute truth.

But does it mean that job-creation programs are definitely a dud? Reuven Brenner, a professor of economics at McGill University in Montreal, had his own ideas on the matter:

> I would say the whole job-creation approach is wrong because the issue for a country is never how many jobs governments create. Governments can always create jobs. Think about communism. There was absolutely no unemployment there — everybody was employed. You can just legislate that everybody who is unemployed gets a salary from the government and presto — they are employed. The unemployment rate was zero point something. How did they do it? Well, everybody had to go to work. If you didn't work you were defined as a hooligan and you entered into the criminal statistics or were put in jail and you were not counted at all. There are other ways in which governments can create employment. If they make a country very poor the country cannot, let's say, import snow-removal equipment, and then the people have to shovel or clean snow with teaspoons. You will have plenty of employment. You will also have a lot of poverty.
>
> Yes, they can always create jobs. They can also enlist people in the army and the unemployment rate will go down.

That's not the issue. The issue is what type of jobs the country is creating, not just whether somebody is employed or not. So first of all, the whole departure point is wrong. Canadians want to prosper. So the question is, are these jobs creating wealth or not?

Just what kind of jobs do governments "create" using taxpayers' money? Most infrastructure jobs, as the Soberman Report pointed out, were low-skill, relatively well-paid construction jobs. In some provinces where the jobless rate was high, infrastructure jobs served as a bridge between two seasons of employment insurance payments.

What's worse, most of the projects financed under the infrastructure program did not appear to teach workers any new skills. Anette, our Manitoba researcher, found a worker who had been employed in an infrastructure project. While his experience cannot be generalized to every job created by the program, the story of Winnipeg worker Shaun Moreau is nevertheless eye opening.

Moreau's welfare agent told him one day about a program called "Community Back to Work." Officials told welfare recipients about a few jobs that would be open to them. Application forms were filled out and then sent through the bureaucracy. Mr. Moreau filed his application form and received a call a few days later — he had landed a general labour job on one of the infrastructure projects.

> Anette: "You were called in for an interview and I guess then you were accepted for the job. Did you receive any formal training after that?"
>
> Shaun: "No, it was a general labour job so training wasn't really necessary. Most people can use a shovel."

Moreau was guaranteed a season's work — which meant that he'd have worked enough weeks to collect employment insurance payments once the job was done. His contract lasted just over 23 weeks. "The type of work we did," Moreau explained, "was general street repair, or replacements in some cases, and sidewalk repair, forming, grating the sand and concrete work." For this sort of low-skilled work, Mr. Moreau was paid a little over $10 an hour — a sum that increased to about $13 an hour roughly midway through the project.

After the project was done Moreau relied on employment insurance payments for a few months, after which he applied at a vocational school to become an electrician and started his apprenticeship with a small company. He said there was no follow-up from Social Services after the infrastructure program was over to see how he was doing and what he was up to. Today he works as an electrician — a job he found without the help of government officials. Anette asked him to rate the government job-creation program in which he took part:

> What I liked most about the program was just that you were working again, you were out doing something, working with a group of individuals … and everybody treated you fairly well. It gives you the confidence to go out and be on your own, find a job again.

We were all happy to see someone off welfare and on a job. But our questions were still unanswered: 1) How could we verify that the number of jobs the government claimed to have created was accurate? 2) Was it a good idea to spend $60,000 of taxpayers' money for each one of those jobs? 3) Did we need a national infrastructure program that ended up costing over $8 billion in order to "create" those jobs?

Despite our mostly unsuccessful attempts to obtain information through the Access to Information law, we assumed we could still get a global number from the federal government because it was compiling the overall statistics. It had been continually releasing numbers to the media on job creation, and politicians kept spouting those numbers when announcing a project or cutting the ribbon after its completion.

Jay managed to lay his hands on some documents that detailed how the federal government tabulated the number of jobs created. It seemed it wasn't happy with the job-creation estimates emerging from the municipalities. A letter dated March 24, 1994, from the Infrastructure Works Office to the federal assistant deputy ministers mentioned the need for a "standard approach for reporting jobs," stating that "this will avoid the problem which was evident in the first projects submitted for approval of poor data from some municipalities, of inconsistent methodologies and also of ignoring important off-site employment associated with supplying infrastructure construction and repair."[8]

In March 1999 three staff members of the Treasury Board told Jay that the federal government had a *secret* method of calculating the job numbers. Yes, that's right — a secret formula. "Why secret?" Jay asked. "Because it is owned by Statistics Canada," was the answer.

Not one to be easily deterred, Jay filed a request with the information commissioner of Canada asking to see the secret formula. How could we check whether the government claims were accurate if we were not allowed to see how the job numbers were compiled? Predictably, the answer Jay received was not the one he was hoping for. In fact, the reasons why he was prevented from seeing the secret formula were so confusing they were brilliant. In essence government officials insisted that the information was available to the public and was not restricted in any way. Except, of course, that we had to pay close to $40,000 for it! As Jay recounted:

> First I was told that the production of the input/output simulations is "one of the products and services offered by Statistics Canada on a cost recovery basis." Then I was told that the models were "custom tailored to particular parameters and specifications requested by Treasury Board," meaning that the models are unique. Treasury Board is the gatekeeper of the information because only Treasury Board officials know the parameters and specifications. The door is firmly closed against my access to the formula because Treasury Board uses an end-user licensing agreement and is permitted to use the product while it remains the property of Statistics Canada.
>
> Statistics Canada developed models that considered direct on-site jobs where the infrastructure work is being done — at the ball stadiums, in the skateboard parks and in the bowling alleys — along with the off-site jobs where the primary resources and services are supplied for the job — the gravel and asphalt companies. Statistics Canada then develops the models by looking at the historical trends that emerge from this kind of investment in six categories, including roads, gas and oil facilities and repair construction. Considering that there are 10 provinces and six categories costing about $700 per model, the Treasury Board was able to save money by combining a few of the similar models in some provinces and ended up paying Statistics Canada $39,000

for the 56 different models. In a nutshell, I needed about $40,000 and my own statistician if I wanted to crack these codes, not to mention the time required to figure out Treasury Board's instructions to Statistics Canada's officials.

Not exactly transparent.

But as I said, Jay is not the kind of guy to give up easily. He thought maybe there was a way around the rules. We could, for instance, compare the input information provided by the Treasury Board with the report by Statistics Canada. Jay thought that if we could see the inputs that were plugged in at the front end, and the result of final report, we could progress a long way in trying to unravel these models.

So he filed an Access request with the Treasury Board for the input information that had been provided to Statistics Canada. We were all anxious to see what he would receive, as you may well imagine.

Get this: after looking at the correspondence between the Treasury Board and Statistics Canada, we inferred that the vital inputs were communicated by word of mouth. That was the end of the paper trail. There was no way we could have those inputs. We were crushed like teenagers in love.

We turned again to Reuven Brenner at McGill. We wanted to know the colour of the bus that had hit us. We wanted to understand what the heck was going on at Statistics Canada, and why it was that we were simply not permitted to verify any of the government's claims regarding job creation. Professor Brenner walked us through it:

They want to give you the illusion that they are doing some scientific work behind [the formula] but ... the job numbers created through this program exactly equal the fraction of the population in Canada by province. Whatever the secret formula is, well, it's just pseudoscience and jargon. That's it.

Could you repeat that please?

The number of jobs created through this program is proportional to the fraction of the population of the provinces within Canada. So, let's say, if Quebec had 25 percent of the population, then 25 percent of the jobs created through the infrastructure program go to Quebec. And if Newfoundland had two percent of the population, then two percent of the jobs are created there. Now, if these jobs had any relationship to wealth creation or any serious consideration other than just a political decision, then there is absolutely no chance that these fractions would be equal. We know the final numbers, and the final numbers of how many jobs were created in each province are political because ... it's impossible that they would be proportional to the population.[9]

Wow.

When you look at the job-creation numbers, they are close enough to the population percentages Professor Brenner mentioned to make you scratch your head in disbelief. Is *this* how we Canadians spend our precious tax dollars when we want to "create" jobs?

In the fall of 1996 then auditor general Denis Desautels reported on his study of the infrastructure program. In a chapter entitled "Lessons Learned" he lists major flaws in the way the federal government calculated the number of jobs created. One of these flaws was the failure to differentiate between full-time and part-time jobs. He also reported that the government's job-creation figures might have been off by as much as 35 percent because as much as one-third of infrastructure funding was devoted to projects that were already slated to go ahead regardless of the program. This lack of incrementality (remember: incremental investment refers to "new" spending) meant the government's job numbers were highly suspect.

Conclusion

In sum, we could not find out who had made decisions to fund particular projects over others. We could not find out which level of government was responsible for doing what. We could not find out who had authorized the spending of public money on the infrastructure program, let alone why. And we could not verify the government's claims as to how many jobs had been created with all that money.

The infrastructure program was simply aimed at repairing Canada's crumbling roads and sewers. It involved the three levels of government in every part of the country. It was a fantastic opportunity for citizens like us to understand, in an empirical, chapter-and-verse sort of way, exactly how Canada is governed today, and to see whether or not accountability was present in the system.

And we could not find anything. (Unless you count the rather big problem of lack of transparency.) We could not even say for certain that there had not been foul play or undue influence in the implementation of the infrastructure program.

We decided to have one more conversation with one of the country's specialists in the field, Canada's former information commissioner John Grace. Mr. Grace had complained in his last annual report to Parliament about the "culture of secrecy" in government. His beef was the notion, apparently omnipresent throughout the bureaucracy, that ordinary citizens could not be trusted with the information they pay for with their taxes:

> Too many public officials cling to the notion that they and not the Access to Information Act should determine what and when information should be dispensed to the unwashed public. Public servants who would be profoundly insulted to be con- sidered anything but law abiding and highly ethical sometimes have had no hesitation in playing fast and loose with access or privacy rights: by destroying an embarrassing memo to file; conducting only the most cursory of searches for records; inflating fees to deter a requester; delaying the response until the staleness of the information blunts any potential damage or embarrassment; and by simply refusing to keep proper records.

We certainly knew a thing or two about delays. The waiting was bad enough, but most maddening were the pitiful results the searches eventual- ly turned up. These unsatisfactory results were almost always a consequence of the generous exemptions allowed the federal government (provincial governments have their own rules) under the Access law. We had no idea that civil servants would be allowed to suppress so many "public" docu- ments using exemption stipulations in the Access to Information Act.

The problem, Mr. Grace told us, is not the fact that there are excep- tions to the Access to Information Act. The problem is *how* bureaucrats apply those exceptions:

> If you ask for information, you have a right to get it unless the government can point specifically to a particular exemption

under the law that enables them to withhold that information. For example, the Access law cannot be used to obtain personal information about other citizens.

The government has some legitimate reasons to exempt, to hold back information having to do with national security. Drug companies can't use the Access law to find the formula that maybe the other company had to submit in order to get approval for a drug. There are many legitimate competitive reasons why information should be withheld, but the exemptions should represent only a small percentage of the vast information holdings of the Government of Canada.

Exemptions are permitted under the law for a number of reasons. The information could be injurious to federal-provincial relations; it could be protected by solicitor-client privilege; it could harm the economic interests of the government or violate an individual's privacy rights. Although all are legitimate in principle, the excessive use of such exceptions was very frustrating and at times downright comical. One letter was turned over to us with only the person's name at the top of the page. All the other words had been censored.

Once, Jay found out that one of his requests about the terms of the federal-provincial agreement between Canada and Quebec had gone all the way up to the PCO (the Privy Council Office) where everything concerning federal-provincial relations is monitored. "The Privy Council," he said, "is a powerful advisory body for Cabinet and is considered the prime minister's administrative agency. My fairly simple request had worked its way to the right hand of the prime minister. I kept reminding myself that I was entitled to see how these decisions were justified. I wasn't after nuclear secrets."

As Mr. Grace told us, roughly 60 percent of all complaints made to the information commissioner are about delays: "Of course, delay is information denied. Timing is important for many of these requests."

Tell us about it.

Another big impediment to accessing government information is the record keeping of bureaucrats. When we did receive documents that were relatively intact, we quickly realized that the civil servants were writing things down using only the vaguest generalities, from the municipal level all the way up to the federal government. The minutes from the meetings of the decision-making committees were so general and incomplete that you couldn't tell what had occurred at the meetings. The only thing you could gather from the minutes was whether a project was approved or not. There was absolutely nothing to indicate that a debate or discussion of any kind actually took place, let alone what was said or by whom.

In John Grace's opinion, what is to blame is this notion that our rulers, our governors, know best:

> That's a vestige from an earlier era when the public was not as educated and perhaps there was some justification for it. Now the public wants to know what the government, whether it be a federal government, provincial or municipal, is up to. That is what Access to Information comes down to.

Parliament passed the Access to Information Act in 1982. It came into effect July 1, 1983. It sets out in general terms the proposition that government-held information should be available to the public as a matter of right, not as a favour. "Access to Information," explained Mr. Grace, "says you shall release all information, except that specifically exempted, and it should be released in due time, within 30 days, not three months, not four months and not in bits and pieces."

I don't think there's any easy solution to the lack of transparency (to say nothing of accountability) in government. All we wanted was to understand how decisions had been made under a program aimed at repairing basic infrastructure. And look where it led us.

During our interview with John Grace in Ottawa, I tried to follow the conversation, but I was distracted by my own thoughts. I kept thinking, "Wow, this guy has actually spent several years banging his head against the very same brick walls that almost drove *me* insane in the relatively short period during which I investigated the infrastructure program. How did he survive? What does he think of all this lack of transparency?"

I emerged from my reverie in time to catch his answer:

> [There is] what I've called a culture of secrecy, and that's the culture that's been handed down to our rulers. Instead of a culture of openness, which I think the times demand and an educated public demands, we are really insulted by this notion that,

"Trust us, we know best. This information might damage the national interest. You aren't able to handle it." It's a paternalistic notion. It is, I think, based perhaps on preservation of power. You know, public servants — good people, most of them — are not highly paid. People want job satisfaction, psychic satisfaction, and there's some, I suppose, satisfaction to be taken, some exclusivity [in saying], "We know this." And of course there's a common fear of embarrassment. You don't want to embarrass the minister, the government, your boss. Unfortunately, in the federal system at least, being known as a person who is open to Access requests, who believes in the concept of transparency, open government, it's not a job-enhancing position to take in government. It becomes "Well, whose side are you on? Are you on the side of these people who want this information or are you on the side of your department who knows best, and we'll decide what goes out?"

Unfortunately, few people in government seem to be on *our* side, the side of the Canadian public.

NOTES

1. Well, not *exactly* ordinary: while it is true that we were not as organized as a professional interest group, we nevertheless had the financial resources to pursue the research. Most of us also had experience in journalism, political science or law. So we were better able to pursue these issues than most ordinary citizens, but like them, we had no inside or institutional advantages.
2. As I said in Chapter 2, we were not criticizing specific projects. We were investigating the decision-making processes that led to their approval and funding.
3. Philip Preville, "How Do I Make an Access to Information Request?" *Saturday Night,* February 24, 2001, p. 16.
4. Former information commissioner John Grace told us that roughly 60 percent of the complaints have to do with delays.

5. Yes, it seems the government did not pay attention to its own report. Not only did it implement Infrastructure II in 1997, but it also promised Infrastructure III in the run-up to the November 2000 federal election.

6. See Richard M. Soberman, *Taking Stock: A Review of the Canada Infrastructure Works Program* (Ottawa: The Canada Infrastructure Works Office, Treasury Board Secretariat, 1996).

7. Canada, Parliament, House of Commons, Standing Committee on Public Accounts, February 20, 1997.

8. George Anderson, Job Creation Estimating Methodology [memorandum to the Ottawa ADMs], March 24, 1994.

9. Population and short-term jobs created under the infrastructure program in each province. British Columbia: 12.13 percent population for 9.84 percent of jobs; Alberta: 9.1 percent of population for 8.53 percent of jobs; Saskatchewan: 3.33 percent of population for 4.91 percent of jobs; Manitoba: 3.69 percent of population for 3.99 percent of jobs; Ontario: 37.14 percent of population for 31.67 percent of jobs; Quebec: 24.94 percent of population for 29.57 percent of jobs; New Brunswick: 2.59 percent of population for 2.76 percent of jobs; Nova Scotia: 3.19 percent of population for 3.9 percent of jobs; Prince Edward Island: 0.46 percent of population for 0.72 percent of jobs; Newfoundland: 2.02 percent of population for 2.24 percent of jobs; Northwest Territories: 0.19 percent of population for 0.28 percent of jobs; Yukon: 0.10 percent of population for 0.13 percent of jobs; First Nations people living on reserves: 1.15 percent of population for 1.45 percent of jobs. Comparisons calculated by Jay Innes. (Source: *National Summary — Approved Projects* [media release], Treasury Board, January 29, 1999, and Statistics Canada for population totals.)

INDEX